THE IRISH IN BRITAIN

The Irish in Britain

Kevin O'Connor

SIDGWICK & JACKSON
LONDON

First published in Great Britain in 1972

Copyright © 1972 by Kevin O'Connor

ISBN 0 283 97868 6

Printed in Great Britain at the St Ann's Press,
Park Road, Altrincham, Cheshire WA14 5QQ
for Sidgwick and Jackson Limited
1 Tavistock Chambers, Bloomsbury Way
London WC1A 2SG

For

Brigid and Margaret O'Connor

Crowds of miserable Irish darken all our towns. The wild Milesian features, looking false ingenuity, restlessness, unreason, misery and mockery salute you on all highways and byways—in his rags and laughing savagery... [the Irishman] is there to undertake all work that can be done by mere strength of hand and back.

—Thomas Carlyle, *Chartism*, 1842

The Irish in Britain live miraculously normal lives in the very difficult circumstances of fitting themselves into a strange environment.

—Peader O'Donnell, *Commission on Emigration and Population Problems*, Dublin 1954

I feel resentful of drunken Irish labour in our streets, of the incredible Irish labour racket operating in favour of the Irish on our building projects, and of the enormous tax-free British cheques cashed at that special Irish pub on Friday.

—Extract from letter to the *Irish Times*, December 1971, from an English reader

Contents

Illustrations

Acknowledgements are due to Chris Smith of the *Observer*, Mr McCaughey, the Radio Times Hulton Picture Library, and the Science Museum, London.

Part One

HOW THE IRISH
CAME TO BRITAIN

1

How the Irish came to Britain

The first trickle which was to become the stream of Irish immigration to Britain can be traced to the twelfth-century Norman-English invasion of Ireland, when Henry II conveniently directed some energetic barons to annex the Ireland of the time. The Irish tribal chiefs, more interested in cousinly squabbles, were easy meat for the mailed and armoured Normans. And the dispossessed Irish set off to lose themselves in the more populous English towns. England, then as now, being no more than a fair day's sail away at the narrowest points of the channel.

England, then as now, had a more developed social structure in the towns and here the Irish refugees lost themselves. Some, with perhaps the beginning of what the native Englishman still sees as Irish cunning and blarney, ingratiated themselves into the Saxon community as street vendors and labourers. The majority, lacking guile and easily discernible as foreign, existed among the riff-raff that seeks warmth and food in any town, to the extent that in 1243 a statute was invoked for the expulsion of Irish beggars, which had the bizarre side-effect of driving the more able into service in the feudal armies. Thus, perhaps, was initiated the tradition of Irish service in the army of the conqueror.

The Irish continued to come across St George's Channel in regular shipments, 'footloose and weary', and to scavenge in the homeland of those who had driven them out of their own hearths. Speaking a different language, coming from a less regimented if besieged tribal society, the majority again sought solace in the lower echelons of the host society. And so, two hundred years after the enactment of the first law to

2

expel Irish beggars, a similar one was passed in 1629, except this time they were called vagrants!

Thus, during the four hundred years between the thirteenth and seventeenth century, the image was formalized of the Irish as slovenly intruders upon the green and pleasant land of England. True, during that time there were bastions of Irish merchants in the main ports who were prosperous, canny and industrious. But following the self–interest of merchants the world over there is little record that they offered much in the way of practical succour to their country-men, preferring no doubt the trader tenet that 'politics and business don't mix'. The ports, of course, were the classic locations where politics and business *did* mix. The ports made money: with the expansion of sea–trade there was a growing demand for warehouses and dealers; in time of war they exacted duty and hostelry from the departing armies and armadas. And in the manner of contemporary gun–runners, it was the colour of a man's money rather than his politics that influenced the merchants of the ports.

The port of Liverpool provides a relevant example. Liverpool owed much of its expansion and prosperity to trade with Ireland and to war with Ireland, and was, in fact, given impetus as a port by King John who needed it as an outlet for his armies to Ireland in the beginning of the thirteenth century – the same century that witnessed the first law for the expulsion of Irish beggars. Four hundred years later, in 1641, in the century that brought in the second law to contain the wandering Irish in Britain, a contemporary historian of Liverpool wrote:

> 'On Saturday, the 23 October, broke out in Ireland the dreadful rebellion and general defection of the Irish, who by a general massacre attempted to extirpate the whole race of Protestants, and in the first three months destroyed 154,000 Protestants, with great cruelty. ... We just briefly mention this horrid massacre, as it had a bad influence on the commerce of Liverpool.'[1]

Commerce was the key to Ireland's besetting problem with England, which was now in the seventeenth century surfing out the oceanic trade routes with man–o'–wars and vessels laden with the exotic goods of the West Indies and the cotton of South Carolina. And Ireland, in her exhausted respites which followed the relentless military defeats by the English, had begun to trade with the West Indies, while at the same time renewing her exports of cattle and dairy produce to Britain. But not for long. The rising merchant–class in Britain felt threatened by expanding Irish trade and in 1670 they lobbied the Government to prevent the importation of Irish products, mainly livestock and dairy produce such as butter. (Three hundred years later, the importation of Irish butter is still a subject of hard Anglo-Irish bargaining.) As a result of the relentless wars upon Ireland, immigrant refugees continued to trickle across to England. They formed few ghettos, but rather took their chances in the rapidly–changing society. The England they came to was one where the feudal structure was disintegrating, and where commerce was the key to advancement; an England sharply divided between 'gentlemen' and others. The feudal society of the rural areas was replaced with that of the towns, where gentlemen wore powdered wigs and knee–length coats over tight breeches. Their ladies moved graciously, if uncomfortably, in equally tight bodices and voluminous skirts; their finery was paid for on the backs of the deprived who huddled in cellars and cramped wooden buildings by earthen streets. Among these the Irish went to ground, distinguished by their accents and appearances, which differed just noticeably from the native inhabitants.

The difference of style of speech was sufficient for the chroniclers of the time. One of the first 'stage Irishmen' appeared in a play produced in London in 1761:

> 'I'm at the Harp and Spinning Wheel,
> in Farthing-Fields, Wapping
> In a room of my own, I hire at ninepence
> A week.'

If that Irish stage character was based on one who had indeed a room of his own, then he was fortunate. Most of his compatriots had more cramped accommodation. As for his rent of ninepence a week, it was no more than a gentleman would pay for a meal of ten dishes. The Irish character proved popular with audiences, which is more than can be recorded for the real-life models who formed a diasporic and furtive influx. There were, of course, exceptions to the general influx, in the persons of individuals of daring and talent who rapidly progressed up the social scale; who regarded English Society as an exploitable commodity for their own advancement. One such vigorous entrepreneur was the playwright Richard Brinsley Sheridan, a Protestant Irishman who in the late 1700s became the most famous playwright in England (while still in his twenties) and whose classic comedies are fruitfully revived to-day.

Displaying that combination of charm and cheek, of verbal fluency and social dexterity with which some talented Irish have regularly—and with some cost to themselves—fascinated the English, Sheridan rapidly assailed the social, literary and political heights of late Restoration England. In a few dazzling decades he managed the Drury Lane Theatre, became a confidant of Prime Ministers and took a Commons seat. And then, with perhaps Irish perversity (always remaining something of an outsider) he threw it all away, while incidentally formulating that tradition of émigré literary entertainment of the English which was subsequently emulated by other Protestant Irishmen in later generations of immigration.

For most of the Irish, however, the towns offered merely drudgery and refuge—and not only to the Irish, but also to the native English cast off from a depressed rural economy. Competition for work led to riots between Irish and native labourers and after such fracas the unlucky injured were charged and sentenced, often to deportation. Some of the Irish found themselves transported in chains to the colonies, and it was poor consolation to know they were helping initiate the world–wide diaspora of their race. It was also of small consolation to know that some of their more business–minded compatriots in the ports earned a hefty living from transportation, the going–rate being in the region of £1,000 per hundred men–in–manacles.

Nevertheless, most survived riots, enmity, and the playwright's flourish. By 1790 the Irish had become established in the ghettos of the major ports of London, Bristol, and Liverpool. In that latter city, in that good year of Our Lord 1790, there were 7,000 cellar dwellings—rank, humid and insanitary—but ready to take the teeming Irish who trekked off the boats from Dublin stunned and sick from the twelve–hour, open–deck crossing.

2

Years of the Scatterin'

W h y in the late 1700s were thousands of Irish leaving Ireland every year? Three causal factors account for the growing numbers of emigrants.

The constant ravages of the English armies had reduced much of the Irish economy and countryside to unproductivity, and the people to insecurity.

The damaged economy was mainly an agricultural one, subject to the whims of weather and season and offering no long–term livelihood to the mainly rural populace.

In spite of this (or perhaps from a sense of desperate tribal survival) the population boomed among a race with a high fertility rate. There was simply insufficient subsistence to support such a rapidly-growing population.

By 1800, emigration to Britain had become a tradition. One critical year later, the Act of Union which merged the two countries under London control, provided increased momentum to this tradition of despair. The Act of Union compounded the influence of irresponsible landlords—increased the number of absentee landowners who resided in Britain on the tithes and rack-rents of a demoralized peasantry in Ireland.

Thus a classic situation of Imperial Colonial exploitation impaled Ireland. Over half her land was owned by absentee Englishmen, while her own native peasantry paid exorbitant rents for meagre shelter and existed on a diet of milk, bread, and potatoes. When the potato failed, as it did with pogrom fatality in 1846 and 1847, panic impetus was given to emigration. Those who had strength to leave the stone and wood hovels trekked to the nearest port and fell aboard, not caring much where the ship might take them to, as long as

7

it was away from blighted Ireland. But to get aboard they had to have money and the cheapest escape was to Britain: threepence for an open-deck passage on one of the new iron ships. Those who made the ports but were without money—and there were thousands—died in the pitch–tar sheds hastily erected for that purpose by the quaysides. Aboard, those who showed signs of disease were abandoned to death. On arrival in England, the demoralized escapees—furtive and in dread—ran the gauntlet of abuse from dockers as they disembarked from ships widely held to be disease–carriers.

The black blight swept most of Ireland, infecting the vital potato to a swollen mush. It is hard now to conceive of the enormity of its ravages, of the townships and hamlets reduced to ruins, of the piled corpses by the roadsides, of the babies born as near–skeletons. 'Death', said an issue of the *Cork Examiner* of 1847 'is in every hovel.'

Why, in 1847, was death in every hovel in Ireland, and not, by contrast, in every hovel in England? The fields of England after all were not immune from the potato blight which swept in from Europe. The answer lay, as do so many Irish answers, with the dictates of British policy towards Ireland. Since the Act of Union of 1801, Ireland had become progressively despoiled under British exploitation. Vast tracts of land had been presented as bribes to those who voted for that Union (including Irish dignitaries of the Catholic Church) and the dispossessed Irish peasantry were reduced to that level wherein all their tillage produce of corn and vegetables were shipped to England as payment for their meagre land holdings. The peasantry thus subsisted on the cheapest vegetable, the potato; their total main dish consisted of potatoes, milk, and bread. At the heights of the Famine, fleets of ships loaded with corn and other agricultural produce daily left Ireland for England. There was a coercive policy of the British Government, reluctant to interfere with the landlord class and needing to maintain the importation of cheap food from Ireland, in order to maintain the impetus of the Industrial Revolution which by then employed six–tenths of Britain's working people. By contrast, nine–tenths of Ireland's population were dependent upon agriculture. All through the Famine, this policy of Britain feeding off the starving Irish was maintained. In the words of an Irish saying of the time, 'Almighty God sent a potato-blight, but the English created a famine'.

To these charges of neglect, not to say genocide, the British administration replied with characteristic stoicism. *The Times* of 17 August 1846 said: 'We are aware that it is necessary to test and weigh an Irish fact before we can admit it to the currency of this more sterling isle.'

When the Government instituted extensive relief measures (while still insisting that the bulk of produce left Ireland every day for England) *The Times* reacted with an essay on the competitive merits of meat versus vegetables:

The Government provided work for a people who love it not ... you might as well give them bonbons ... For our own part we regard the potato blight as a blessing. When the Celts once cease to be potatophagi, they must become carnivorous. With the taste of meats will grow the appetite for them: with the appetite, the readiness to earn them. (22 September 1846)

One million Irish died of disease and starvation. One million escaped aboard the 'coffin ships'; half of these came to Britain. Through the port of Liverpool in one year passed three hundred thousand ravaged Irish; to Glasgow journeyed fifty thousand; to Manchester went twenty thousand; to London two hundred and fifty thousand. They arrived in such throngs, were so cowed, suspicious and superstitious that they created instant ghettos in their areas of settlement. A year after the Famine struck, and while it still raged in Ireland, the British cities of Manchester, Glasgow, and London had all sprouted their 'Little Irelands'.

Today, one hundred and fifty years after the Famine diaspora, the districts thus settled are still identified as Irish: Hammersmith, Camden Town, Paddington, and Islington in London; the Gorbals in Glasgow; Stockport, and the Newtown areas of Manchester and Cardiff; Scotland Road in Liverpool. From the entry port of Liverpool they joined the road from Holyhead, heading for London. The influences of that trek are apparent today, in that on or near the route of Watling Street were the growing towns of Wolverhampton, Coventry, and Luton, towns which today hold strong Irish contingents. And where the Great North Road came into London was the then pleasant and leafy village of Camden. (So much for the popular legend which ascribes Camden Town's Irishness to being as far from Euston Station as an Irishman can travel carrying two suitcases on a Friday night!)

Eastward from the port of Bristol came the Great West Road and along this route was the town of Reading and further in towards London the village of Hammersmith, and in both of these areas the fearful, fleeing Irish settled. They came, too, into the Port of London and into the district of Rosemary Lane in the East End which soon came to be known as 'Little Ireland'. The areas in which they settled were, for the most part, the decaying districts of the towns and cities festering with latent fever. Contemporary accounts are colourful and unflattering: 'The Irish were crowded together with all their native habits of filth and indolence', wrote the author of a fever report.

Where the remnants of the Great North Road straggled beyond Camden towards London was The Rookeries, a square-mile of dilapidated tenements which the Irish colonized with all the fervour of plague–fleeing rats. Of this district (near the site of today's aptly–named Warren Street Station) the Novelist Charles Dickens, wrote in *Oliver Twist*:

> The sole places that seemed to prosper amid the general
> blight of the place were the public houses, and in them the
> lowest orders of the Irish were wrangling with might and
> main . . . drunken men and women positively wallowing in
> filth and from several of the doorways great ill–looking
> fellows were cautiously emerging, bound to all appearances
> on no very well disposed or harmless errands.

Dickens, as a newspaper reporter, would have accepted the general image of the Irish as unkempt and sinister. That this image was widespread may be noted from the following description of a London settlement by Mayhew, an equally avid chronicler of social conditions, who perceived, however, that the process of immigration could also bring a measure of self–improvement. Mayhew wrote:

In the houses that I entered were traces of household care and neatness that I little expected to have seen. The cupboard fastened in the corner of the room, and stocked with mugs and cups, the mantelpiece with images ... gave an air of comfort that *strangely disagreed with the reports of the cabins in 'Old Ireland'*.

Not indeed, that there was any dearth of references to cabins—and pigs. The Irish were reckoned to look after their pigs, 'as an Arab his horse'. Which is a relevant analogy, for the pig was economically vital to the Irishman, being as much as he could rear for food and profit in his meagre mud–and–stone holding in Ireland. Many brought young pigs with them and slept with them for warmth on the open-deck crossing. The pig survived on scavenging and thus could be reared cheaply. But certainly the grā (love) for pigs–in–the–kitchen originated part of the image of the Irish immigrant. (And though we may be bemused in hindsight now, it is equally relevant to record that the abusive term of 'pig' for policeman is said to have come from the predominance of the emigrant Irish in the police forces of American cities.) It is relevant, too, to mention that the Irish served to draw off onto themselves the sort of resentment that any people or society will display towards that element which is alien to the general native fabric. The Britain of the early-to-middle 1800s lumbered into the cauldron of the iron and steel revolution on gross human inequalities. The general demeaning conditions of the labouring populace, the child-labour and the short wretched life–span of the working classes have been sufficiently well–documented. In Liverpool in 1840, the average age of death was: gentry and professional persons 35 years; tradesmen and their families 22 years; labourers, mechanics and servants 15 years. This was the contemporary urban grimness which the famine-fleeing Irish came to, that they might survive. No surprise then, that the natives reacted with vehemence to the sickly hordes who came raggedly teeming from the coffin–ships of faint hope. Even Frederick Engels, the supporter of Karl Marx and of working-class sanctity, had a cold eye for the Irish immigrant. 'His crudity', said Engels, 'places him little above the savage.'

Engels's attitude was echoed by most contemporary social commentators, journalists, and newspaper cartoonists. More bitterly was it acted upon by pockets of workers, so that lone Irishmen were regularly set upon and beaten. And in the high–flown religious rhetoric of the time, when the native English held strong Protestant views, the Irish bore the Cain–mark of being Catholic. Hardly surprising then that they clung to their ghettos, wherein they retained some semblance of their culture, spoke Irish and brewed drink, smoked pipes and fought with sticks; all marks of savagery to the natives on the outside.

In Scotland the antagonism was more fierce, again lent bitter barb by clear-cut religious differences. Irish Catholics were the subject of mass hostility, but not Irish Protestants who were accepted by the Scots with a respect reserved for missionaries who have survived in the land of the savage. This particularly applied to Irish Protestants from the north of Ireland, accepted by the Scots as of themselves.

The rest of the Irish—the majority—were the object of abuse, which reached absurd proportions in Glasgow. There, a favourite street game was known as 'Hunting the Barneys', and involved rounding up the Irish who were then required to utter public pronunciations of such words as 'peas' and 'tea'. The rural–originating Irish pronounced (and still do) these nouns as 'paze' and 'tay'. In Glasgow in the 1820s such utterances were the signal for communal and vicious beatings of the Irish.

And yet they survived. Tight, clannish, looking up to their natural tribal leaders the priests—who often quelled rows with the hard knob of a blackthorn stick—the low–sized, sickly Irish put down their weak, grudging roots into the insanitary slums and into the maw of the Industrial Revolution. In a way, the timing of the Industrial Revolution

was fortunate for the Irish. It allowed them the full rein of
energy and work, and its circumstances dictated some element
of common toil with the native population. The new mills
for cotton, coal, and iron and steel were hungry for human
fodder. The English workers came reluctantly from the
countryside and found their new life as strange as did the
Irish. The irony was that at the same time as Ireland's back
was broken by the Great Famine and its despoilation of
people, England was on the brim of riches beyond the dreams
of even the most avaricious fledgling capitalist.

The key to this booming wealth was the evolution of
mechanical ability; the means whereby iron and steel could
be functionally fashioned, which in turn developed the
methods to extract it in massive quantities from the hitherto
harbouring earth. Impetus begat impetus with the steam
locomotive spanning iron bridges to traverse the country to
reach expanding ports, where larger steam-driven ships
ferried the export goods to the captive markets of the colonies.

Twenty years after the Great Famine, during which two
million Irish left their blighted shores, England was the
greatest industrial nation in the known world. Half the world's
coal was raised from her pits; half the world's textiles came
from the Lancashire mills; one third of the known world's
output of manufactured goods travelled on British ships.

The 'mere Irish' of the raddled ghettos were not untouched
by this burgeoning wealth and activity. In the ripening coalfields of Wales, in the cotton-mills of Manchester, in the ports
of London and of Liverpool, they worked fiercely, furtively,
and with the urgent awareness that work, in its most critical
sense, meant survival. Most dramatic, perhaps, was their
contribution to the railways, which were so vital in opening
up new dimensions of territory, and transport of people and
goods.

> And drill, ye terriers drill
> Drill, ye terriers, drill
> It's work all day for sugar in your tay
> Down beyond the railway.

The time of heaviest Irish emigration, the 1840s, was also

the time of the railways and the Industrial Revolution. In a sense, they begat each other. Railways were the 'high fashion' of the times, needed alike by the State and the capitalists. From 1822 to the end of the century 20,000 miles of railway passage were dug, hewed and blasted across England. Immense undertakings of engineering skill and navvy grime, the railways were privately financed for profit. Accordingly, work schedules were tight; the toughness of the contractors and entrepreneurs (many of whom were bankrupted by unforeseen difficulties) was exceeded only by that of the navvies who blasted and burrowed across England the transport system we take for granted today. There were little or no mechanical aids – the age was not that advanced – and the navvies by the forties had evolved to a skilled toughness of intent and behaviour which lent them a special glamour of reputation, separate from that of general labourers.

For the Irish who took to navvying, the 10,000 miles of railway track which they helped build in the latter 1840s had a significant effect upon them. To begin with, they had to overcome the resentment of the native navvies: for all the handed-down myths that the Irish built the railways, rarely did they exceed 30 per cent of the overall navvy force. Resentment against them was strong and pitched battles occurred between navvy groups of opposing nationalities. The English navvy was a craftsman and often a countryman who took immense pride in his calling, fancying himself as something of an engineer (which he often needed to be) and resenting the Irish intruder, who in the words of a ballad:

> When work grew scarce and bread was dear
> and wages lessened too,
> the Irish hordes were bidders here
> our half-paid work to do.

The most vicious hostility came from the gangs of Scottish workmen who, with pick-handles at the ready, tramped across the country to flay the Irish, burn their huts and terrorize their women. After one such expedition, the *Scottish Herald* reported that: 'It was truly pitiable to see several of the wives of the Irish labourers sitting, at short distance from the blazing huts, in the midst of a few articles of furniture which they were able to save from the flames, wrapped up in the cloaks peculiar to their country, and watching with melancholy countenances the gradual demolition of their humble dwellings.'

As a result of this sort of regular attack, Irish navvies never worked alongside the Scots and only rarely with the English. Almost always they worked in their own clannish group away from the other two belligerent nationalities. The only recorded instance of harmony between Irish and the natives appears to have been with the Cornish and Devon miners who were engaged in tunnel blasting on the Midland railways in 1870.

Even when kept separate, the Irish could be recognized at a distance by their dress; the men by their widespread use of the smoking pipe (an piob) and liking for black serge waistcoats, the women by their black shawly cloaks. Closer to, the approaching Englishman would know them by their lolling walk and finally by the lilt of Irish, which to the English observer sounded like a babble of Italian.

They were, like the Irish today, by turns peaceful and troublesome. Many commentators of the time found them withdrawn, quiet and eager only to work, stay with their own and remit money home so that others might join them. Other observers found them fearsome and sinister. Timing of the observers' visits may have accounted for the divergence. Certainly the peaceful Irish of a Sunday would present less passive exteriors on the Monday which saw a spate of fly-posting which sloganed:

NOTICE IS GIVEN

that all the Irish men on the line
of railway in Fife Share must be off
the ground and out of the country on
Monday 11th of this month or else we
must by the strength of our armes
and a good pick shaft, put them off.
Yours humbel servants, Schots men.

It is worth remembering that various forces in the Britain of the mid 1800s combined to focus emotion upon the Irish. Famine–caused immigration from Ireland was at its height, so that ragged refugee Irish were obvious in all locations of employment. And because the Irish were refugees from that 'starvation' they were poorly equipped physically as well as being carriers of disease (a fever introduced into Manchester by the Irish in 1846 was active years afterwards). The 'Irish Question' was a regular issue in Parliament and word–of–mouth accounts of trouble in Ireland doubtless became inflated to hysterical proportions in the work camps. Finally, the general pressure towards the restoration of Catholicism in Britain was given numerical leverage by the Irish influx, providing severe provocation to Scots Presbyterians in particular. Thus the most vicious battles of the railway era were between Irish and Scots. The perceptive writer, Terry Coleman, has provided a reconstruction of one such pitched encounter which took place at Gorebridge, near Edinburgh, in February 1846:

'At Gorebridge, about ten miles south of Edinburgh, the gangs of Irish navvies had been paid in a pub. Many of them were angry because they had received less than they thought was due to them: they were illiterate and had not kept any count of the past month's tickets which all mounted up and consumed a great part of their wages. But they had enough to get drunk on. In the course of the long drinking evening a packman arrived at the village and went to the pub. The Irish were there, by now thoroughly happy, but still with some money left. Would they like, asked the packman, to see some watches, good watches? All right, said the navvies, and two watches were handed round for inspection. That was the last the packman saw of them. When he asked for the watches back they laughed at him. What watches? There was no point in arguing with a gang of drunken Irishmen, so the packman went to the village police station and complained. Two of the carousing navvies were dragged out of the pub, arrested, and locked in one of the cells at the station.

'For a while the Irish muttered to each other. Look what

those damned Scots policemen had done. The news spread, the
navvies gathered, the muttering grew into a universal grievance
against the generality of damned Scots, and someone began
a collection, which his colleagues rapidly took up, of all the
pickaxes, bludgeons, and hedge–bills to be found. By half
past one in the morning there were nearly 200 Irishmen,
suitably armed, and they moved off to make their represen-
tations to the police.

'The two policemen who happened to be in charge at the
time, Sergeant Brown and Constable Christie, tried at first to
reason with the men and to prevent them from entering, but
they soon saw that the Irishmen were determined and that it
was impossible to stand against such a mob. For fear of their
lives they gave way, and even then Sergeant Brown had his
left arm disabled by a blow with the back of an axe. The
rabble crowded into the station and found the cells. One of
the mob then ordered the sergeant to unlock the prisoners
and, when he refused, presented a pistol at his head and
threatened to kill him there and then unless he did what he
was told. The sergeant still refused, so the men left him alone
and pulled down the cell door themselves, freed the two
prisoners, and marched off with them towards Fushie Bridge,
about half a mile off.

'They had gone only a short distance when they met two
policemen on their ordinary round, the district constable,
Richard Pace, and John Veitch of the railway police. Pace
and Veitch heard the rabble and tried to save themselves by
hiding in a hedge, but it was too late. They were seen, pounced
on, and dragged out. Veitch escaped in the scramble, but
Pace was knocked senseless by a severe blow on the head from
a pick handle. The Irishmen laughed at him, put the boot in
as he lay on the ground, and then left him. He was all but
dead. Two lads who had heard the shouts of the mob from a
distance, crept up when the navvies had gone, and found the
constable lying on the road only a hundred yards or so from
his own house. The alarm was given, Pace was carried home,
and a doctor got out of bed. But Pace was so badly hurt that
he never spoke again, and at six o'clock on Sunday evening
he died. He was a married man, but had no children. Veitch,

B

the policeman who got away, was hurt about the head, but was well enough to go back to duty on Monday. By mid-morning on Sunday the news had reached Edinburgh, where Alfred List, superintendent of the county police, hastily consulted with the sheriff and agreed to send a contingent of the county force, together with twenty-four of the city police, to Gorebridge. This force reached the village at midday but by then the rioters had dispersed and all was quiet.

'But not for long. News of the outrages had also reached the navvies working on a stretch of the same line to the south, and these men were Scots, mostly Highlanders, and English. They hated the Irish, and resolved to extirpate the Paddies, burn their huts and be rid of them at last. All this was to be done, so it was afterwards explained, to avenge the dead policeman, who was a Scot. The rest of Sunday was given up to planning and drinking and threatening, and then, early on the Monday morning, the Scots and English moved, more than 1,000 of them by now, towards the Irish huts. The local policeman saw this gathering and sent a rider off to Edinburgh. Another detachment of the city police was sent out from Edinburg in a coach and four, and the cavalry at Piershill barracks were alerted. But by this time the navvies were well on their way, gathering numbers as they went. At Newbattle paper mills, which they reached between nine and ten o'clock, they were joined by 150 of the Marquis of Lothian's colliers, also keen to rout the Irish. There were now nearly 1,500 on the march, and they drew themselves up in proper array, with colours flying, with a piper and bugler at their head, and armed with bludgeons and shafts which they had wrenched from the hammers and other tools belonging to the railway, not one of which remained intact.

'At Chrichton Muir, to the north, the Irish waited until they saw how many were coming against them, and then they fled, some leaving their families behind. So when the Scots reached the first huts they were unopposed. They smashed and burned, and the huts of wood and turf were soon so many heaps of smouldering ruins. On again they went, and burned the huts near Borthwick Castle. One solitary row, that nearest Edinburgh, was all that now remained, and this was soon levelled with the rest.'[2]

But if the Irish endured much – and they also occasionally retaliated when favoured by superior numbers—the railway work at least uprooted some of them from the more decayed ghettos and led them to find new ones of marginally improved comfort.

The other significant effect was to involve the Irish more fully in the general labour market of which the pick–and–shovel navvies were princes. It was the first communal involvement of the 'diasporic Irish' to the expanding land of their adoption. Afterwards, they would reply to prejudice: 'We built your railways.'

Not quite true, of course. The railways were built by English, Scots, and Irish, in roughly those proportions. But the implication was, that if the criticism did not cease, the Irish would set about dismantling the lot!

3

Of Settling and Assimilation

The time has come when the Irish
population must either be improved
a little, or else exterminated.
—Carlyle, 1840

Though most of the arterial railways were built between 1840
and 1860, the time–span which saw a million Irish arrive in
Britain, the immigrants' work activity was by no means
dominated by the railways. The Irish found employment
wherever they were; in the coalfields of Scotland and South
Wales, in the cotton–mills of the Midlands, in the expanding
ports of East London. Even before the mass migration from
the Great Famine, they had begun to eke out some sort of
grudging acceptance from the native population, an acceptance
punctuated by outbursts of hostility such as the Gordon Riots
of 1780 and the agricultural disturbances in the Scotland of
1830. These, and other expressions of communal antagonism,
were almost always occasioned by a combination of factors in
the eyes of the natives: The Irish were strike-breakers who
would gladly work for a lower wage. Their religion was an 'alien'
one. They were dirty, unkempt, fractious and separate.

Yet the grudging acceptance they were accorded by the end
of the 1800s was partly due to this quality of 'separateness'. The
Irish had become the 'Oirish' of familiarity, part of the fabric
of the times. In the building trade, 'Dublin tricks' was rhyming
slang for bricks; in Lancashire a small village of stone houses
was named Padiaham, reputedly because:

Paddy I am and Paddy I be
an' I name this place after me.

A look at how the Irish were assimilated into the East End of London, by then the melting–pot of immigration, is salutary. Here the Irish developed two earned identities of some respect, those of tunnel diggers and street vendors. The men worked in the nearby docks which were being furiously expanded to cope with the outpouring exports of the Industrial Revolution, while their wives and children sold trinkets and fruit from barrows in the streets. The first tunnel under the Thames, engineered by that visionary partnership of Brunel, father and son, took twenty years in the burrowing and lining and was largely dug by the Irish. Brunel had devised a massive burrowing iron shield, housing thirty–six excavators in precarious protection, which rooted in at the Neanderthal–clay, untouched since the world's creation. Behind each excavator, back–to–back, a bricklayer cemented the brickwork lining of the tunnel. When finished, the tunnel was something of a historic marvel and apart from the engineering genius of its conception, the Irish were accorded some local respect for their part in its construction.

But even with such dramatic expansion of the ports, work in the East End was not regularly plentiful. Men queued outside dock gates, in the hope of a day's unloading, or outside contractors' huts. The appearance of a foreman, as Mayhew recorded in *London Labour and the London Poor* was the signal for 'the scuffling and scrambling forth of countless hands, high in the air, to catch the eye of him whose voice may give them work. All are shouting. Some cry aloud his surname, some his Christian name, others call out their own names to remind him they are there. Now the appeal is made in Irish blarney—now in broken English . . . the scuffle being made the fiercer by the knowledge that hundreds must be left to idle the day out in want.'

For those who had to idle the day out, the street–selling of their wives and sons made the vital difference. We have seen how some element of the emigrants had clung to a tradition of street–selling. It is easy to understand why, for the trade initially required little beyond a ready ingratiating tongue allied to a nagging persistence. This was sufficient for the immigrant wives and children to earn some sort of living. But

as Mayhew observed, they displayed other hardy qualities as
well, which soon brought them to dominate street trading and
wean away its monopoly from that other great immigrant
influx, the Jews. Mayhew noted:

> The Irish boy could live harder than the Jew – often in his
> own country he subsisted on a stolen turnip a day – he
> could lodge harder – lodge for a penny a night in any
> noisesome den, or sleep in the open air, which is seldom
> done by the Jew boy... Thus, as the Munster or
> Connaught boy could live on less... the Hebrew youths
> were displaced by the Irish in the street orange trade.

So two immigrant communities – both fleeing from versions
of racial persecution – found themselves competing for an
economic foothold in new and alien territory. Mutual
antagonism was intensified by later waves of Jewish exiles,
who, fleeing from the homicidal antics of Catholic monarchs
in Europe, found their way blocked by Irish Catholics in
Britain! Not surprisingly, by the 1870s, the East End had
become sharply divided between Jewish and Irish districts,
with the cultural inheritances brought in their baggages, so
to speak, by both diasporic races being too strong to allow
any easy tolerance of the other. The Irish were in Saffron Hill,
Drury Lane, Cromer Street; the Jews colonized from the
Whitechapel Road up into Goodman's Fields and Petticoat
Lane. New families who attempted to set up home in the
'wrong' area were stoned out and away. In the event the
Jews won. Increasing waves of Jewish immigrants from Russia
made inroads into 'Irish' territory, grafted back most of the
street trade. But if the Irish met with rigidity from the Jews,
there was less resistance from the 'natives' of the melting–pot
East End. In the forty years after the Famine, the Irish had
become established and accepted, albeit still with the air of
'separateness' about their settlement. In an era which saw
Blacks, Chinese, Lithuanian and Russian Jews fuse into the
society of the East End, the Irish put their tribal names over
shops and pubs, on the sides of street–stalls and on to the
stages of the music halls. The music halls were perhaps the
most obvious signs of growing acceptance, for on the other

side of the orchestra and footlights were glorified and sentimentalized the issues and personalities of the day. With such songs as
'God Bless the Prince of Wales' (and his Molls), went
'Paddy's Wedding' and the 'Limerick Races'. In these temples
of racy song–and–dance the working-class thronged with a
wry ear to hear that 'It's the rich wat get the pleasure, and
the poor wat gets the blame', to be followed by 'Pat's Leather
Breeches', both equally sentimentalized tributes to themselves
and to the immigrant 'Oirish'. By the turn of the century, so
popular had Irish Acts become in the music-halls that the
redoubtable Scotsman, Harry Lauder, initially presented
himself as Irish, as did many other would–be stars of the
gas–and–gaiters limelight. The Irish penchant for the colourful turn of phrase, the fey response to questioning and the
self-mocking seriousness (all marks of an oppressed people),
provided ideal material for music–hall jokes and songs. Such
folk-hero status suited well the mass of emigrants. For it was
the thin end of the wedge towards general acceptance. Only
later, in the early 1900s, would the later emigrants cast a
cold eye on such stage–status and abhor an image compounded
of sentimentality, buffoonery, ingratiating idiocy, and lumber-
ing cunning.

George Bernard Shaw was one such critic of the
stage–image, as were the middle–class Irish civil servants who
came in appreciable numbers in the early 1900s to occupy
desk–space in the Imperial civil service. But neither they,
nor Shaw, had had to survive the immigrant trauma of the
eighteen–forties, fifties, sixties, seventies, in a burgeoning
vigorous East End, where a stray Irishman in his labouring
moulskins (corduroys) never knew whether the local men in
the pub would greet him with sullenness, satire—or a fist in
his begrimed face. For him, the music-hall caricature meant
at least acceptance, if occasionally derisory and dangerously
sentimental acceptance. But then, the mythology of 'Oirish-
ness' was created by the native English on the basis of real
life impressions (happily nudged–on by the objects of caricature). The tragedy—on a broader scale—was that the
appealing image of impoverished (if cunning) peasantry was
to survive beyond the time of its validity. This caricature

meant that the English did not take the Irish seriously. In the East End of the nineteenth century, regularly lurching towards the brink of racial pogrom, this refusal to be taken seriously was welcomed by the struggling–to–survive Irish.

That the mythology so mutually conspired to then survives today at various levels of English life—such as Government— is one of the sinister legacies of the Irish diaspora of the 1840s onwards. (Even today, a hundred years after the creative circumstances of that mythology, English visitors who return from Ireland in a state of mild surprise at the cohesive society they encounter are often unaware that they have had to over- come an image of the Irish inherent in their own British up- bringing—an image rooted in the nineteenth century and created for mutual ease by both English and Irish.)

If the Irish of the East End were thus agreeable to being exalted on stage, their compatriots in other areas of the country were less flexible. In the textile mills of the Midlands, the Irish became prominent in affairs of industrial agitation; they were quick to seize on disputes. The lists of those arrested following such agitation contained a disproportionate amount of Irish names, and in evidence to an enquiry in 1835, a cotton manufacturer exclaimed that 'it was a notorious fact that in the small hand–loom mills where many Irish were employed, there have been more turn–outs than in any other...' In the same enquiry it was also declared that 'the Irish were the talkers and ringleaders on all occasions of trouble'.

So while in London the quality of 'separateness' had been chronicled on the stage, in the Midlands the same separateness was recorded in the industrial agitation of the times. Add to these characteristics the obvious Irish influence on the growth of Roman Catholicism in England, and one has the defining characteristics of an alien body in a host society.

Yet it was an alien body of growing substance and impact. The Irish were increasingly represented at all labouring levels of English society: in the factories and ports, in the harvest fields of Scotland, in the collieries of Wales and further south to the farms of Kent, and beyond to Devon and Cornwall. In the growing towns they were increasingly becoming the leg–up of the rising bourgeoisie, as domestic servants and

maids. A contemporary account of one such classic Irish maid–
servant poignantly perceives the quality of separateness, and
not least the differences of language and culture. The incident
was recounted by a distressed gentlewoman to that social
reporter, Mayhew.

'... and if the Irish hussy didn't spill a whole basinful of
water on the floor, and then actually seemed in no way
inclined to wipe up the slop on the boards. So I begged
she should take a cloth and do it immediately. But the minx
replied: 'Oh, sure and don't it always soak in, in my
country.' Which was a good deal more than I felt I ought
to put up with. So I told her very plainly, 'that her
country... must be a filthy, dirty place and only fit for
pigs to wallow in.' No sooner were the words out of my
mouth, than she turned round sharp upon me, and shrieking
out 'Hoo! Hubbaboo!' seized the kitchen carving knife and
brandishing it over her head cried out, 'Hurrah for ould
Ireland, the first jim of the say – and a yard of cowld steel
for them as spakes agin' her!'

The media of the times are littered with such accounts of
the feckless, fey, fighting Irish. Reporters in search of 'human
interest' stories crowded the courts when cases involving Irish
were heard, for they could be sure of choice actions and
phraseology with which to regale their readers. Male defendants were invariably described as a broth of a boy, as fine a
sprig as ever flourished in the Ould Emerald Isle, or introduced
along the lines of: Big Barney, Bould Mike, Poor Paddy.

This was the newspaper equivalent of the music-hall
compounded in equal parts of affection, fear and racial
superiority. Certainly the living conditions of the Irish—at the
bottom of the pile—allied to their growing numbers provided
ample material for the courts. By 1861, one quarter of the
population of Liverpool was Irish-born, yet Irish names
accounted for over half the offences of assault, attack, inebriation, disturbance of the peace. By 1871, over 800,000 Irish-
born lived in the 'Little Irelands' of Britain, and most of
these ghettoes were shunned by 'respectable' citizens and the
police entered only in numbers.

B*

Fighting was the principle law-breaking activity, sanctified among the inhabitants to the level of a national pastime. Most fighting occurred over inter–county rivalry, i.e. that particular Irish county of origin of any particular group. The week–days and evenings were convivial enough, with just the occasional clouting to reassure them of the national identity. Come pay-day and evening the tap–rooms of the ghettos filled with muscly men—and wiry ones too—and the virtues of one county would be trotted out by one group, in good–natured bonhomie to tease another group. All would be tolerant as the high-point of 'the crack' was reached; colourful abuse tossed to and fro, century-old legends resurrected, the sporting prowess of one county set against that of the other, until the high-point was passed and the gamut of verbal warfare exhausted. Then came the descent into boredom and into brooding melancholia, the inherited sense of despair and uselessness, the imaginations raggedly tempestuous now from the competitive drinking and, a sudden bunched fist would crack into one fellow's face and in seconds the place was in turmoil. This was the pattern of disturbances, unintelligible to the outsider, totally understood and condoned by those within.

The unfortunate ale–house keeper would send a runner for the Peelers and some mornings later a bewildered magistrate would have recounted to him the historical virtues of one distant Irish county versus another. When one remembers that the ghettos contained immigrants from each of Ireland's thirty-two counties and that many of the immigrants identified more with a particular county, or even with a particular parish within a county, than with being Irish, one can sense something of the magistrate's bewilderment and of the hostility and bewilderment of the authorities to the frequent fights which characterized the ghettos. The identity which the sense of belonging gave an otherwise anonymous labourer was so powerful, that certain ale-houses were exclusively this county or that. The new-arrived Irishman, on entering, would shortly be asked: 'What countyman are you?' and on the geographical location of his answer balanced his future well-being for the evening.

The Irish ghettos throughout the country were, as has

been noted, inevitably in the more decaying, dilapidated districts of the cities. Street upon street of raddled houses, families living in single-rooms, excrement piled by communal dumps in the gutters, washing strung across the cobbled and dirt-street; the whole overhung by insularity, insecurity and deep suspicion of outsiders. These were the conditions of the immigrants. The men dressed in serge trousers and waistcoats, the women in shawls and long-skirts, the children most often in hand–me–down rags.

The one with some 'book–learning' parleyed with officialdom on behalf of the ghetto, another who had been a cobbler continued his trade here. The majority of the men having tilled small plots in rural Ireland found no such continuation here and formed the bulk of those who had to adapt to labouring and navvying, to porterage and factoring. Some, having come from areas of large tillage, dealt in fruit and vegetables; their names can still be seen on the store-fronts of London's Covent Garden Market. Some, having had no trade in depressed Ireland, developed entrepreneurial instincts in the ghettoes, as keepers of doss-houses and truck-shops (general and beer stores). These more sprightly spirits grew rich on their compatriots. One such rented a house for 2s. 6d. per week and let out twenty beds at ninepence a week per bed. In such houses beds were double-let, with a man on day–shift taking over from one on night–work and men usually slept two to a mattress. Sanitation was by slop–bucket and washing–water came from a trough or pump. The women, in respites from child-bearing, worked in factories and warehouses and the more artistic developed a flourishing side-line in base-coinage, the system whereby their men-folk and others exchanged the lawful currency for counterfeit coinage of higher apparent value.

Irish ghettos became centres for the manufacture and passing of such coinage, the authorities being hindered by the solidarity and clannishness within. Overall, the priests were the most powerful individuals, being political as well as religious leaders of the settlements. The priests, by their academic training and by the nature of the tribal offices they held, served as liaison officers between the ghettos and the outside world. Looked up to with mystical and superstitious awe, called upon to arbitrate upon disagreements and to quell disturbances, they wielded a power equalled only by their religious counterparts in Wales and Scotland. As the visiting French writer, Faucher, noted: 'Police arrangements would be quite inefficient among the Irish, unless supported by *ghostly influence*.'

4

Of Priests, Politicians and People

That matters of religion and politics were irretrievably inter-
woven into the lives of the wary immigrants of the nineteenth century is, essentially, a commentary on the proximity
of Ireland to Britain. The previous century's Protestant
supremacy of power in England inevitably rippled outwards to
the immediate, and unwilling, colony of Ireland. The degree of
Ireland's unwillingness was critical. Whereas the anti–Catholic
Penal Laws of the late eighteenth century had reduced the
Catholic religion to a meagre foothold in Britain, in Ireland by
contrast the laws were vigorously, if deviously, resisted. Not
entirely on abstract theological grounds, one is tempted to
think, but rather on the racial reaction that they were imposed
by the English. (The corollary today, as expressed in a letter
to *The Times* in 1971, is that if England insisted on being
Catholic, the Irish would react by turning Protestant!)

Thus the majority of Irish immigrants of the nineteenth-
century ghettos were defiantly Catholic, settling as aliens into
a country which had scant sympathy for that belief. Their
coming, paradoxically, was to revitalize the Roman Catholic
Church in Britain and to become the single most influential
factor in the restoration of Catholicism to Britain, to the extent
that numerous Catholic historians see in the ravages of famine
nothing less than the hard hand of 'Divine Providence' in
restoring the Faith to England.

Before the Irish influx, the English Catholics were a depleted
minority. They hardly numbered more than fifty thousand in
a population of seven million, sustained only by the dual
political influence of the Catholic aristocracy – the Old English

29

Catholics of landed estate power and the tiny communities attached to embassies of Continental countries.

As early as 1792, thirty years after a Chancellor for Ireland had declared that 'the laws of Ireland do not presume a Catholic to exist',[3] the Irish had opened their first semi-public church in London—predictably enough named St. Patrick's—in Soho. The priest was Father O'Leary, a Franciscan friar, who ministered to the Irish of the area and to those who came gratefully flocking from the scattered hamlets about the capital. The opening of the church—formerly an entertainments hall of some notoriety—followed directly upon the passing of the Catholic Relief Bill, tolerating public Catholic worship. The Government measures towards restoration were not disinterested; across from France wafted the acrid whiff of Revolution while in Britain pressure to relent came from worthy sources (the parliamentarian Burke had earlier pleaded before the Throne for the right of private Catholic worship).

There was too, perhaps, the calculation in respect of the immigrant Irish that it was better to alleviate historical antagonism in view of the impending Act of Union. In the event, the tremulous emerging English Catholics were only too eager to abide by the colonial policies of the Government in return for gradual restoration. The loyalty of Catholics was very much in question, and subsequently to be an issue of much bitterness between Church authorities and later Governments. Certainly Catholic support—in Ireland and Britain—was canvassed for the Act of Union. The founding Father O'Leary was among those who addressed his London–Irish congregation in favour of the measure.

The whip-hand of the State was to have a profound developing effect. Because of the suspect loyalty of Catholics, and the later fear of 'Papal Aggression', the bishops were intensely wary of offending the Government on matters of foreign policy. In the developing uneasy relations, reaction of the English bishops towards policy on Ireland would be a matter requiring the utmost delicacy of reaction: following the Act of Union of 1801, discriminatory legislation against Catholics lay heavy on the statute books.

Against such political uncertainties did the Roman Church

gather expansion and recruits in Britain. Led by the scions of the old English Catholic families, given vent by the learned converts from Anglicanism, and depending most critically on the diehard loyalty of the Irish immigrants, the Catholic Faith revived and flourished. By the mid–1800s the promise, almost a century earlier of the lonely Bishop Challenor—'There will be a new people'—appeared in retrospect to be a prophecy. By 1852, the convert and intellectual, John Henry Newman, was able to declare: 'The past has returned, the dead lives . . . the English Church was not, and the English Church is once again. . . . It is the coming of the Second Spring.' Underlining the Second Spring were the multitudes of refugees from the Great Famine in Ireland who flocked into the towns and cities of the Industrial Revolution of nineteenth-century Britain.

They brought with them those elements of national culture which successive imperial persecutions had failed to eradicate: the gutteral Irish language in which reposed their history as spoken fables, and their nourished version of the Church of Rome. To the latter they, for the most part, clung covetously. Their defined nationalism made them suspicious of English priests, and though they contributed with almost excessive generosity to the building of the new churches[4] (the Catholic Church was not allowed to occupy even derelict Established Church premises) they were wary of public prominence at services but rather gathered at the back of the churches during worship. With their own Irish priests they were more relaxed and confidential, seeing them as temporal rather than spiritual spokesman for their own affairs. A contemporary description of one of those priests of the people is enlightening: 'He had powdered hair, white cravat, knee-breeches, black stockings and silver-buckled shoes . . . being a tall and powerfully built man his appearance at once commanded respect and admiration. He settled disputes among his people by his very presence, or where that failed, with the threat of a heavy stick which was the regular companion of his visits among them.'[5]

Inevitably, the growth of such cohesive Irish Catholic strength provoked hostile reaction among the sections of native working-classes. Scotland and, to a lesser extent, Wales, witnessed many periodic outbreaks of violence directed against the émigrés. In Cardiff, the first Catholic Church since the Reformation was consecrated in 1842, the backbone of its congregation being the Irish who had settled in the Newtown area of the docks.[6] The growth of this community was so devoutly strong as to provoke, six years later, a mob who attacked the church and ransacked the Irish cabins of the area.

The motivation for such attacks was hardly theological, but rather the reaction which any human native society expresses towards the presence of an 'alien' body with which it feels threatened. That the native society should thus feel threatened points, in the final analysis, towards an economic reaction. It was the misfortune of the Irish—no strangers themselves to attacking the entry of a foreign body upon native hearth— that the Britain they came to in the eighteen-thirties, forties and fifties was one of already simmering unrest, due in the main to the dislocative effects of the Industrial Revolution which threatened the welfare of an agricultural-based proletariat.

It was not uncommon for new agricultural machinery to be set upon and destroyed by rural workers fearful for their livelihood. Farm-workers engaged in a campaign of atrition for better wages and conditions, burning hay-ricks and threshing machines and generally being at violent loggerheads with the landowners. It was, ironically, the same sort of war which the Irish immigrants had lost in Ireland. Now as they arrived in Britain their very numbers provided one more threatening factor to the natives, who saw the émigrés as an economic and political intimidation. The high–point of such antagonism were the Stockport Riots of 1852, which compounded the elements of economic fear, racial fear and religious hysteria among an already intimidated native population. The political prompt to the disorder was the re–establishment from Rome of the Catholic Hierarchy in Britain in 1850, wherein, in the decree of Pope Pius IX, the Church 'may again flourish in the Kingdom of England'.

The move was reacted to with alarm by the Government who passed the Ecclesiastical Titles Bill. Among other preventions, the Bill forbade the carrying of Catholic insignia and banners in public places, resulting in bitterness among Catholics. The Irish Catholics, already defiant and resentful

in religion by the ferocity of penal repression in Ireland, were
put in a defensive mood. Stockport, an outlying town of
Manchester, provided the flashpoint! In the county of
Lancashire of the 1850s lived almost a quarter of the immigrant
Irish population of Britain, drawn there by the weaving and
spinning employment of the cotton mills. The town of
Stockport held a strong Irish ghetto which had grown from
a mere 300 at the beginning of the century to over 8,000 by
1852. They were, by contemporary accounts, an unruly community in a state of tense antagonism with the native English
workers. Existing in overcrowded, crumbling houses, along
Rock Row and Bridge Street, the Irish were 'likely to turn out
at a moment's notice and set on the first person they met and
maltreat him cruelly'.

Thus the Irish of Stockport, surly and quick to take offence:
their impending annual procession in June 1852, coming some
days after the Royal Proclamation of the Ecclesiastical Titles
Bill, saw opposing forces ranged. The following account cap-
tures the atmosphere and sequence of what ensued:

'The Royal Proclamation had been hailed as a sectarian
triumph by the lower classes and they had boasted that they
would see the proclamation enforced in the case of the young
red-necked scholars, as they termed the Roman Catholic
children.

The Irish decided that the annual meeting of scholars was
not a procession of the sort interdicted and published their
resolve to make their demonstration as usual. There was great
excitement on the subject and it was said that the authorities
thought of preventing the school gathering; but when the day
came, the Protestants seemed less excited and the schools were
allowed to make their procession without interruption. The
Sunday passed off without disturbance, a fact which may have
been due to the presence of a body of strong Irishmen who
accompanied the procession, which studiously avoided any R.C.
insignia.

The whole incident appeared to be closed when on the
following day many personal encounters began to take place
between Irish and English parties originating from a disturbance

in a beerhouse. On Tuesday there were still more evident signs of commotion and some street fights occurred during which the windows of St Peter's school (Protestant) were broken. This led to a general melée in St Peter's Square when some stones were thrown through the windows of Alderman Graham's house. Rioting then became general and serious; so fierce in fact that the police could not suppress it. The rioting lasted spasmodically for three days, being finally put down by dint of the combined efforts of the police who managed to hold the chief body of the rioters in check and of the mayor and magistrates who meanwhile had assembled and sworn in some hundreds of special constables. The civil power had just gained the upper hand when a body of military also turned out and the riots were quelled. In retaliation for the assault on St Peter's School by the Irish, the English had turned the fight into an attack on the houses and chapels of the Irish. The mob attacked an Irish-owned beerhouse, first demolishing the furniture and breaking the windows; finally attempting to set it on fire. They then proceeded to treat the houses on Rock Row and down Bridge Street in like manner reducing them to complete wrecks. The mob next demolished Edgeley Chapel and the minister's house, nothing being left but the bare walls. The chapel of St Michael in King Street was then gutted; here also everything was destroyed. The list of seriously wounded comprised sixty-seven persons named; one man was killed and some others died of injuries received. Hundreds of Irish had fled from the town and slept in the fields for weeks, fearing to return to their homes lest there should be a renewal of disturbances.'⁷

*   *   *

Although a religious procession provided the spark, the underlying causes were essentially territorial, and possibly economic. Nevertheless, the Stockport Riots—widely reported—fuelled the propaganda of Catholic and anti-Catholic interests. The Catholic paper the *Tablet* concluded that the disturbances were fostered by ruling political interests in pursuit of middle-class Protestant-Anglican votes. By contrast, the local *Stock-*

port Advertiser put forward a view which, given the situation and the siege-mentality of the Irish, appears more credible. The paper judged that the riots were caused: 'in a great measure by the taunting, insulting course adopted by the Irish, particularly in taunting the English as cowards for not preventing the procession of the Irish Scholars on the Sunday before the disturbance took place'.

Though mild in comparison to the contemporary conflagration in Ulster, the riots predictably reinforced the trenchant Catholicism of the Irish. As the cyclic prosecutions of English dominance had helped define Irish consciousness over the centuries, so equally did the Stockport Riots confirm the immigrants in their sense of dual identity, that of being Irish *and* Catholic in Britain. The riots, in effect, strengthened and increased Irish loyalty to the Church, for at the time less than half the émigrés were regular attenders at Catholic services; a 'leakage' was demonstrated in the year preceding the Stockport affair, when a religious census showed less than half the Irish population to be in attendance at Sunday Mass. While in some measure qualifying circumstances arose from lack of accessible churches, seven-day working week and ghetto insularity, the 'leakage' away from the Church must also count.

In London, for instance, the census showed a Mass attendance of 27,494 persons, whereas the Irish-born population of the region was 81,453 persons. Undoubtedly the alienating lingering effects of the Penal Laws accounted for some of this lapsing, as did the deeply-ingrained insularity which made many suspicious of attending service at an *English* Catholic Church, ministered to by *English* priests. Though the émigrés formed the rank-and-file of congregations, the officers so to speak, i.e. the priests, were mainly English, drawn from the aristocratic English families who had held on to the Faith through the protective political-cum-class structure of the era. The Irish were often uneasy with such men and the priests, though manifestly devout, were uneasy with the Irish.

The awkward relations were patently historical and inhibited the confidential participation of the immigrants with the growth of the Church. Given the weight of their recent colonial sufferings at the hands of the English, the mass of Irish workers could hardly be expected to fully identify with a church command-structure dominated by English upper–class enthusiasts. Most priests attempted to 'bridge the gap', but the differences were severe. Wrote a Catholic essayist, of that formative period:

> We may smile at the Irish Biddy selling her cabbages at the corner of the market–place; but the telling of her beads as she sat behind her stall, and the patience she has shown in her poverty, are not the least influence that has told for good in the regeneration of England.[8]

Not the least of the diplomatic successes of the Church leaders was in fusing the disparate elements of the Irish Catholic immigrants into the general corpus of a church administered by an English hierarchy. True, of course, that a substantial minority of that hierarchy was of Irish or Anglo–Irish origin by the mid 1800s. But equally true that Irish–born priests were provided with sparse encouragement to ascend the administrative structure beyond the level of parish priest. The dictates of 'political sensitivity' mitigated against their promotion, the Irish priests being, by and large, identified with an immigrant grouping politically antagonistic to the Establishment. The very physical import of throngs of Irish labouring classes crowding the new and restored churches must have been seen in terms of a political power–base with resultant flutterings of unease among a Government coping with various fronts of potential disturbance—in the rural areas with agitation for higher wages, in the cities with pressure for electoral reform, and in Ireland with the periodic sparks to the powder-keg of nationalism.

Therefore the stance of the Catholic Church in England—leaning over backward to assure the Government of patriotic loyalty—was a required consolation to the Government. The stance was less consoling to the mass of immigrants and to their native priests who were nevertheless bound by one of the prime tenets of their ministry, that of obedience to their (English) superiors. So the Irish grudgingly accepted their paradoxical status of having the most numbers—but the least power—in the growth of Catholicism in Britain.

This latter position was, anyway, one which they were historically conditioned to and which perversely provided a measure of comfortable identity to the politically apathetic, but which was to be challenged by two of the leading Irish activists upon the British political arena of the 1800s. From the Act of Union flowed most of the subsequent evils of Anglo–Irish history while to the refugee Irish in Britain in the early part of the century it seemed as if that Act had made manifestly evil their state.

At its door did they bitterly lay their condition of poverty, deprivation and hostility to their religion. Had they been less nationalistically insular they would have noted that the lot of the native English working classes was little better, that in fact both communities were equally victim to the class–cum–capital structure of the 1800s, and both about to be steamrollered under the weight of the Industrial Revolution. Instead, with that penchant for self–pity and hindsight, they saw only the rural stretches of the land from which they had been driven by the Act of Union, by famine and by absentee English landlords. Thus when Daniel O'Connell, orator extra-ordinary and the leading Irish political figure of the 1820s made it his stated goal to repeal the Act of Union, the abject emigrants in Britain saw in him their potential saviour.

> What is an Englishman made for, but to work?
> What is an Irishman made for, but to sit at
> his cabin door, read O'Connell's speeches and
> abuse the English.
>
> *The Times*, 21 January 1847

There is no demonstrable reason why more Repeal would have improved their lot unless with the optimism of despair they assumed that the return of an Irish Parliament would also mean their return to the homeland, that an Irish Parliament would have shipped them all back to the fondly imagined green and pleasant pastures.

O'Connell's appeal, in fact, lay with the power of his personality: was that of the demigod. A burly, massive man, a lawyer trained in France and Britain, his vituperative lashings of his opponents in the British House of Commons endeared him to the emigrants. For them, he was 'The Liberator' who freed them psychologically from their own communal weight of inadequacy. Yet equally he pandered to and encouraged their sense of narrow penitential nationalism. Huddled in the ghettos, they gathered about the few of their number who could read to hear tell of O'Connell's verbal exploits in Parliament, of how he damned Disraeli as 'Being Descended from the bad thief who died upon the Cross', of how opposition to Repeal was 'mere vomit upon the floor of the House', of how he 'would drive a coach and four through any act of British Parliament'. When Lord John Russell attempted to cajole him with arch humour, O'Connell reacted that Russell's smile 'was like the glint of moonlight upon the brass plate of a coffin'.

The émigrés thronged the highways to catch a glimpse of him, and, literally tried to touch the hem of his cloak. His influence among them was immense: he held them in tow and in thrall, attracting the fervour of religious momentum, for in harness with his campaign for Repeal went opposition to the Oath which prevented any Catholic of integrity from assuming a seat in Parliament. The Oath did not, however, bar O'Connell, an avowed devout Catholic, from Parliament. Neither did his Catholicism exercise restraint upon his sexual generosity, for he fathered a number of illegitimate children.

His championing of the underdog did not extend towards his tenants on his Kerry estate during the ravages of the Famine. His radicalism, such as it was, was on behalf of the Catholic landed gentry and not for the peasantry, and certainly not for the dispossessed peasantry now floundering in the maw of the Industrial Revolution in Britain. Yet through his dogged and devious resistance to British Rule in Ireland, he became for that dispossessed peasantry a figure of adulation. And because he became for them a figure of adulation, the anti–Catholic and anti–Irish hostility of the time was focalized upon his own person. Said the *Glasgow Courier* upon his impending visit: 'His arrival is exciting the most intense interest among the whole inhabitants of the lower stews of the ciy.'

Twenty years later, the Presbyterian powers of Glasgow were vainly passing resolutions to repeal the Act of Catholic Emancipation, for O'Connell's parliamentary brilliance did succeed in removing this discriminatory Oath. Repeal of the Union, however, had to await repeal in the blood and cordite of the General Post Office in Dublin in 1916. Nevertheless, O'Connell's activity was the earliest radical influence upon the Irish in Britain. He removed the parliamentary stigma against their religion, he sustained their deep emotional attachment to the ideal of an independent Ireland, and most important of all, in the early dark days of the diaspora, when the Irish lay huddled in the ghettos of Britain, O'Connell provided the beckoning voice of hope in the wilderness. But his impact was essentially a calculated one of regarding them as parliamentary gun-fodder. His preoccupations and anxieties were essentially on behalf of Catholic landed gentry of Ireland. It is a comment upon ... structure ... me that the peasants so identified ... him such massive support ... build O'Connell's campaign fund ... Irish peasantry.

But because nationalism and hatred of England was in the air, only later would the more perceptive among them realize that to replace the English Protestant landowner with an Irish Catholic version was not necessarily to improve matters. Though the Irish devoted centuries of rebellion towards the demolition of military manifestations of British Imperial rule, they heartily absorbed the underlying caste tenets upon which that rule was dependent.)

Chartism, by contrast, sought to eradicate the feudal–capitalistic basis of Imperialism by organizing the working classes of Ireland and England. It sought to harness the nationalistic and peasant unrest in Ireland with the unrest of sections of the British proletariat. One of the doctrine's most militant protagonists was Feargus O'Connor who sat in the Commons as M.P. for Cork. O'Connor was originally a protegé of Daniel O'Connell, but their companionship broke on a mixture of personal spleen and differing political philosophies. O'Connor had effective sympathy with the labouring class. O'Connell had little. O'Connor wanted to unite Irish and

English workers for their joint betterment. O'Connell, a land-owner, feared the organization of the working–classes.

In the Irish tradition, they parted with acrimony. While O'Connell played on the immigrants' nostalgia for an independent Catholic Ireland, O'Connor campaigned for their well–being in Britain, for their alleviation from the slums and sweat shops of the Industrial Revolution. A man of similar physical assertion to O'Connell – he once thumped Lord Palmerston – and of equal sexual democracy, O'Connor's political analysis moved along Marxist interpretations (he was among the first to publish Marx). A founder of the Radical Association and the most demanding of the Chartists, he stomped the country in support of his People's Charter. He directed working–class agitation towards the formation of trade unions, addressing meetings in the ghettos of the crammed towns and cities of England. From a minority of the Irish he garnished support, most strongly in the industrial Midlands and North. A workers' paper launched in Yorkshire soon ex-ceeded the sales of the *Manchester Guardian* of the time. A personality of oratorial and physical impact, with flowing red hair and sonorous voice he was, in an age of theatrical impact, the first meaningful political leader of the Irish in Britain; the first to harness a potential that, had it not been deflected by the cause of nationalism in Ireland, could have been functionally and politically significant. For the Irish, rough, turbulent and insular though they were, had some sense of political involve-ment, particularly in Lancashire and the North of England.

Though pressure of the Radical Association brought about some electoral reforms in 1830—increased parliamentary representation for the upper middle classes—O'Connor campaigned further for labouring–class representation of which class the émigré Irish formed a weighty proportion. After raids by the authorities on Chartist clubs in Manchester, it was reported that: 'The police arrested the following persons: James Leach, Daniel Donovan, Joseph Finnegan, Patrick Devlin, Michael Carrigan ....' As an afterthought the report added: 'There were also some English names among those arrested.'

Though the Government had, with unease, granted limited

electoral reform, O'Connor's demands for across–the–board representation had too much of the tenor of real dilution of upper–class power. As such it was violently opposed by the landed interests of the day, including the figure of 'The Liberator', Daniel O'Connell. And in campaigning for immigrant Irish support, *O'Connell's* supporters tried repeatedly to wreck *O'Connor's* meetings, or as one activist put it: 'We drove the Chartists out of the hall four times. We thrashed them and passed our own resolutions.' Thus was the continuing divisiveness of the Irish maintained, making them, with chronic inevitability, their own worst enemies. O'Connell's Irish supporters became so competent at breaking up the Chartist meetings, that they were hired as bully–boys by property and landowner interests of the day to thwart Chartist gatherings. O'Connell's antagonism severely limited Irish support for measures which would have immeasurably improved the lot of the immigrant Irish in Britain beyond anything that Repeal of the Union would have wrought. Not only were the Irish labourers who broke up Chartist meetings acting against their own real material interests but the splintering of the Irish community reduced the potential they had to become a viable political influence in terms of ethnic weight.

Nevertheless, Feargus O'Connor's achievement in uniting sections of the English and Irish proletariat—even for a short few years—was an epic one and unequalled since. Yet like Parnell, generations later, O'Connor in his hour of need was abandoned by the very multitudes he sought to uplift. The leader who, with half–a–million workers at his back, once faced the Duke of Wellington's militia, was finally rendered harmless. The Government incarcerated him within a lunatic asylum.

By then, anyway, the dual if divided efforts of the 'two O's' had brought about substantial political advances in the lot of the Irish in Britain. Daniel O'Connell had removed the discriminatory Oath preventing Catholic participation in Parliament, and secured the general measures of Catholic Emancipation, endemic to the restoration and growth of Catholicism in Britain. A weighty caste–mark upon the Irish had been removed. Feargus O'Connor had also improved their lot, not as an ethnic minority, but by directing the labouring classes toward the formation of trade unions. Under this dual impact of O'Connell and O'Connor, therefore, the community had by the 1860s become socially and politically advanced upon its previous state.

For some, however, the pace of constitutionalism was too slow and invited the emergence of the mailed fist that lurks in the vicinity of most Irish arguments. This time they were called the Fenians, precursor of the Republicanism known today as the Irish Republican Army. Like Republicanism today, it garnered but a tiny minority of support from among the 'exiles' (predictably, areas of strong immigrant insularity such as districts of Lancashire and Glasgow provided the bulk of adherents). Springing from a cultural recall of a pre-Christian Gaelic Ireland, the Fenians took their name and inspiration from the mythological tribal guardians of that utopian time—Na Fianna. Modelled thus on figures of heroic classical proportions who were reputed to leap mountains and battle with the Gods, the Fenians of the late nineteenth-century Irish ghettos had to compromise at the more mundane level of arms-drilling and conspiratorial whisper of armed uprising of the Irish in Britain.

It was never really on, of course. The mass of the immigrants, as we have seen, were too impaled upon the rigours of day–to–day survival. The former peasantry of Ireland, now the urban peasants of British cities, were never conditioned to mass insurrection. Rather were they conditioned to improve their lot by guile, labour, and petty dishonesty. The minority who were politicized were drawn off into the radical and con- stitutional movements of Feargus O'Connor and Daniel O'Connell. Thus when Fenian activists were arrested in Man- chester in 1867, there was no 'storming of the city gates' by revolutionary hordes from the Newtown ghetto. Instead, there was the storming of a prison van, incurring the death of a constable. His colleagues promptly saved the Irish killers from a mob bent on biblical vengence in the streets. In November of that year three men, Allen, Larkin, and O'Brien were hung for the murder of the policeman and have become enshrined in Republican conscience as the 'Manchester Martyrs'. In the month following their execution, another incompetent attempt involving explosives was made to rescue a Fenian from London's Clerkenwell prison. The prisoner survived the excessive explosion of a barrel of gunpowder, but a row of nearby houses were demolished and twelve occupants died. This time there were no handy perpetrators for mob vengeance, but that evening Irishmen were pulled out of pubs in the East End and assured of their racial identity in nearby alleyways. The Clerkenwell episode provided a predictable cathartic shock. Ghetto support for the Fenians dwindled overnight, native public opinion was outraged, Irish labourers were without jobs and the Government, among other reactions, founded an undercover branch of the constabulary to maintain surveillance over Irish and other political subversives. (Today, over a hundred years later, the lineal descendants of that police branch, now known as MI5, keep a shadowing relationship with the other lineal descendants of the Fenians, the I.R.A.)

But as well as being the precursor of Republicanism, the short-lived tenure of the Fenians among the immigrants had significance in another direction. For the year of the Fenian activity was also the year in which the vote was first given to the urban proletariat, thereby allowing the Irish in Britain to capitalize on their ghetto-grouping. Constitutionalism, as opposed to the political leverage of physical force, was given an energetic push forward. By the 1870s, the urban masses of which they were most a part had begun to group *en bloc* behind leaders who curried their vote. By the advent of Charles Stewart Parnell, the Irish were able to influence voting patterns. And by that time, too, they had become a secondary power in the Catholic Church, to the extent that Cardinal Manning in 1882 over-stated: 'I have given up working for the people of England, to work for the Irish occupation in England.' The twin emancipations of the community were to dovetail upon the personality of the next radical leader of Irish opinion, Charles Stewart Parnell, who in the House of Commons headed the Repeal of the Union agitation, now titled as Home Rule.

Whereas O'Connell before him had drawn little from among the Irish in Britain beyond crowd support and emotional energy for Repeal of the Union, the post-famine influx of the

1850s had produced, by the 1880s, the first ethnic voting bloc. The county of Lancashire again provided the bulk of Irish support. The politician and journalist, T. P. O'Connor, representing the Scotland Road constituency of Liverpool put his vote behind Parnell. Michael Davitt, a product of Irish settlements in industrial Lancashire was a vigorous propagandist within the immigrant communities. So vociferous and potent was immigrant agitation that the English hierarchy were prevailed upon to cool the political passions of their Irish congregations during the outbreaks of agrarian violence in Ireland. (During which landlords and their families were murdered by sections of the Irish peasantry.)

The platform this time was Home Rule for Ireland and reform of the land–rents, and this latter issue held great emotional sway with the immigrants who were, for the most part, victims of such rents. They identified with Parnell to the extent of depriving the Liberal party of seats in the General Election of 1885. This election saw the emergence of the ethnic vote among the Irish in Britain. The balance of power in the subsequent Parliament lay with the Liverpool–Irish constituency seat represented by T. P. O'Connor.[9] Faced with this unique 'ethnic lever' in Britain, the Government introduced various measures which considerably aided the lot of Irish peasantry in Ireland, giving them in the first instance grants to purchase their smallholdings and thus free themselves of the crippling rack–rents. By 1890, these measures had encouraged 200,000 Irish smallholders to purchase their lots, a modest social and economic revolution which most Irish historians (and militants) prefer to ignore.

By 1890, in fact, a number of extensive measures had drastically improved the lot of Ireland in areas of academic institutions, social welfare, rural education. In Britain, correspondingly, the means of the émigrés had considerably improved. The fortuitous power of T. P. O'Connor's 'ethnic vote' in the 1885 Government gave vent to a nationwide organizing of the Irish in Britain. By 1890, the Irish National League had 630 branches throughout Britain—approximately the number of seats in Parliament—which lobbied for the immigrant vote on the issue of Home Rule. And though its registered members were but a minute proportion of the émigré population, less than ½ per cent, the fact of its existence and direction raised the political consciousness of the immigrants. In Parliament, the Irish party headed by Parnell wrung concession upon concession for the welfare of Ireland, and seemed on the brink of achieving that misty political objective which Irish hearts hankered for, namely the creation of an independent self–governing island. The projection seemed thus set fair, as the watershed year of 1890 approached. And then the strains under the currents smashed upwards, released by a few trite phrases in a London Divorce Court of December 1889. Parnell was named as the co–respondent in the matrimonial action of a junior member of his own party, Captain O'Shea.

Though Parnell's liaison with the lovely Kitty O'Shea was exposed and manipulated by his political enemies, in the final analysis it was the political immaturity of his own Irish followers which cut him down. Following the Divorce Court evidence, which made light of the fact that Kitty O'Shea had been living apart from her husband for ten years, almost everybody went for Parnell: the British Establishment, the Catholic Hierarchies of England and Ireland (politically united for once), his own 'inner cabinet' (including T. P. O'Connor), ranting parish priests all over Ireland (long jealous of his sway over the people) all tore into the wounded chief. In Scotland, a country of higher political consciousness among the immigrants, their paper, the *Glasgow Observer*, put the matter into more valid political perspective:

What all the enemies of Ireland failed to do against Mr Parnell he has done for himself. It is hard to write calmly on the black business. Pity and anger strive for the mastery in the mind of every friend of the Irish cause. Pity for Parnell in his weakness and infatuation, pity for Ireland in her betrayed position. This is the first feeling, but in truth it is impossible to keep down anger at the whole dirty, disgraceful business. Mr Parnell knew the risk he was running. He knew that he was the man at the helm, guiding the barque of Erin's hopes through troubled waters. He has deliberately handed over his charge to the enemy. He has endangered by his folly the cause entrusted to his care, and caused the tinge of shame to mantle the faces of twenty millions of admiring followers. It is a terrible fall. We are at last face to face with the cause of Mr Parnell's peculiar conduct during the last few years. He made innumerable appointments and never kept them. His party met to decide most vital matters. Parnell was absent. He neglected his duties as leader. His followers neglected theirs, for did he not set the example? And now it is all out. Mrs O'Shea was of more importance than honour, or duty, or rectitude. Oh! the pity of it! Seldom has a tale been told in the Divorce Court showing more duplicity, trickery, meanness and folly. A great political leader climbing out of back windows, shuffling about in disguises, changing his name, and generally acting like an arrant fool, while all the time watchful eyes were on him, noting his shifts and tricks, waiting the hour to make them public property. Was there ever a more humiliating revelation of man's littleness? For years this matter has been a bone of discord in the Irish party. We can all recollect how it nearly led to a breach in the ranks over the Galway episode. But no warning was heeded. Mr Parnell was mad, and in his madness he has continued to this day.

The paper itself conducted a poll of readers' opinions which declared itself firmly outraged, and in cohort with the British Establishment, desired his political demise. Unable to combat the hysteria of opposition, Parnell unwillingly obliged. Thus, not for the first time, did Catholic Irish puritanism conspire against the salient political interests of the Irish people. A year later the former 'uncrowned King of Ireland'—now dethroned—was dead.

It is worth briefly to pause here and survey the progress, other than religious–political, which the Irish community had made in its settlement in Britain. Though the overthrow and death of Parnell sundered political cohesion among the émigrés, that very cohesion of the 1880s reflected the underlying cohesion of the community. By then the settlements of the ghettos had taken root, and become an accepted feature of the larger towns and cities. The offspring of the Famine refugees, the first–and–second–generation Irish, had asserted themselves in the community, providing social and political leadership and, with their English accents and Irish temperament, acted as an *explanatory continuum* between the Irish communities and the world outside. By the 1890s, the Irish had notched up their first century of free-flowing immigration into Britain. During that era they formed the largest ethnic minority and the most separate single sub-group of the poor. In the reports of social workers and welfare committees, they were identified with the poor—it could be hazarded that either the poor gave the Irish a bad name or the Irish gave the poor a bad name. Certainly the dovetailing of the two strata was profound and was reflected in the figures for court convictions and imprisonments in which both the Irish and poor scored, disproportionate to their numbers.

But as the completion of the nineteenth century witnessed an improvement in the lot of the poor, so did it witness similar improvement in the émigrés. The Irish had put down their roots in the festering ghettos of the early 1800s (when communal excrement was sold for manure, fetid tenements were without ventilation—there being a tax on windows—corpses lay 'waked' for weeks and at any hour of the day at least a third of the male inhabitants were in a state of inebriation). They had grown with and survived the Industrial Revolution of the mid–century and had, towards the end of that century, the heady glory of holding the balance of power in the Government of the day. They had been touched and improved by the powerful social forces of the era: the development of the railways, the Ten–Hour–Day Factory Act, the compulsory education of children, and the increase in life expectancy. Their era was punctuated by the Gordon Riots at the beginning (which left them fearful); the Stockport Riots in the middle (which left them defiant); and the Fenian explosions of 1867 which, while begetting Republicanism, left the majority unconverted to that prejudice. By the watershed year of 1890 the Irish had become a settled community. The effects of (among other pressures) their own voting weight in key areas had induced the Liberal–Conservative Government towards a benevolent Irish policy. One result was an immense improvement in economic conditions in Ireland, and a consequent reduction in immigration to Britain (these were also years of heavy alternative emigration to America).

By the end of the nineteenth century, they had become a settled community of nearly a million among a population of thirty million. They had developed their own internal structure of community support, based mainly on the publican and priest. They had built their enormous Catholic churches, published their own newspapers,[10] and were making tentative excursions out of their ghettos. In the cities they worked as labourers, costermongers, and street vendors. A lesser number continued in the privileged caste of navvies, while thousands sated their fighting–lust in the British Army Regiments which spearheaded actions in the Crimea and in Southern Africa. Whilst in the upper echelons of Society, mavericks such as Bernard Shaw and Frank Harris continued that tradition whereby Irish literati instructed the English as to how the English might best behave themselves.

As a diasporic people, the trauma of the Famine Scattering was behind them. The twin prongs of fate and colonialism, so to speak, had pitch–forked the Irish from the home–hearth across St George's Channel into the domain of the titular enemy. Both they and the surprised native needed a breathing space to recover from that shock encounter. The benevolent fading of the nineteenth century, with political peace in Ireland and no great social unrest in Britain, provided them both at least with that measure of racial relaxation.

Part Two

ONWARDS FROM THE 1900s

5

Onwards from the 1900s

The period of comparative political calm between both countries which marked the opening years of the twentieth century disguised, and encouraged, the growth of what was to become the most potent force in Anglo–Irish relations, namely Irish nationalism. Surface impressions were benevolent and deceptive. Under pressure from the Irish Parliamentary party at Westminster, the Government's attitude to Ireland brought about increased land purchase by former tenants and a modest alleviation of the grim social conditions. The Irish version of the Industrial Revolution had brought increased employment to the towns, with a consequent drop in emigration to Britain to a level of around 20,000 annually, the lowest level since before the Famine. Much of the emergent political strains in English society were mirrored in Ireland, with one salient difference. Whereas in England the new feudal structure of the industrially new rich had produced the simmering discontents of left-wing socialism, in Ireland the same rebellious philosophies now being nurtured were directed *nationalistically*. Whereas in England these forces found expression through the formation of the Labour party, opposed to the indigenous rulieng class, in Ireland the same dissident attitudes were directed against a ruling class which happened to be English in its manifestations and personnel. Whereas in England the movers of the new socialism were scornful of the social habits and mores of the 'ruling class', so in Ireland were the formulators of similar reaction scornful of similar characteristics, which were most simply seen as manifestations of *English* rule.

Accordingly, the creators of Ireland's reactionary equivalent

to the British radical resentment formulated a caste of Gaelic
Ireland attitudes. The ancient books of legend and folklore
were plundered for manifestations of an exclusive Irish culture.

Any symbol imagined to be native Irish was 'in', everything
symbolic of the English/Anglo Saxon was 'out'. The movement
became known as the Gaelic Revival, and like most such
obsessions, was initially developed by middle–class cultural
enthusiasts—of whom one, Douglas Hyde, was to become the
first President of the Irish Free State—who ranged wide (and
sometimes ridiculous) in their search for symbols which might
awaken the peasantry to 'their true destiny'. The peasantry
initially reacted with scepticism to the urban obsessives who
came among them, sometimes dressed in cassocks and head-
bands and crossed leggings which they fondly imagined to
have been the attire of ancient Irish heroes of mythology. A
concept of racial Irish purity was preached by devotees such as
Constance Gore–Booth and Douglas Hyde, themselves of
Anglo–Saxon landed ancestry. A relic of the monastic Middle
Ages, the Ardagh Chalice, became the model for an athletic
prize, to be competed for by exponents of 'Gaelic Games'.

Under such bizarre tutelage, the movement nevertheless
flourished. The Gaelic Athletic Association, set up to foster
contests 'racy of the soil' flourished in an atmosphere of discovered nationalism. No member of the British Crown Forces
(military) or of the Royal Irish Constabulary (which consisted
mainly of Irishmen) were allowed to participate in its contests,
a rule which still applies in Northern Ireland. Douglas Hyde,
who claimed to dream in Gaelic, was to found the Gaelic
League and to become first President of the Free State declared
by armed rebellion in 1916. Many of those who baptized the
new state in cordite were graduates of Constance Gore–Booth's
Fianna Eireann boy scouts, militantly modelled on the
mythological Fianna.

Thus was a revolutionary movement in Ireland formed,
fashioned and fired by recourse to malleable legend and appeal
to concepts of racial nationhood revived from the embers of
folklore memory which had survived successive conquests. The
Gaelic Revival, which incorporated the Gaelic Athletic
Association, the Gaelic League, Sinn Fein (Ourselves Alone),

and the Irish Republican Brotherhood, pivoted on two splendid ironies—the fact that much of the Revival was initially conceived by stalwarts of the Anglo–Irish class and the fact that its subsequent flowering was due in no little measure to the increased literacy and education brought about by a benevolent British Government. (Today, a valid contemporary allusion lies in the fact that many of the Ulster–born prime movers of the Civil Rights agitation, which sparked Ulster to its present conflagration, were beneficiaries of a British-subsidized higher education which, had they been born in the Irish Republic, would probably have been denied them.)

Among a section of the immigrants to Britain, the Gaelic Revival took firm root. The first few years of the 1900s, while showing a drastic reduction in immigrant numbers, were also witness to the influx of what, for want of a better term, one may call middle–class immigrants. They came particularly to join the Civil Service, having sat the entrance examinations in Ireland. Two such candidates, who were later to become prominent in affairs in Ireland, were Michael Collins and Sam Maguire. The writers Padraic O'Conaire and Peadar Kearney (an uncle of the famous Behan brothers) worked in London at the same time, and the poet William Butler Yeats lived in Kensington and presided over the Irish Literary Society—in London! In nearby West Kensington, Michael Collins lodged with his sister, was employed in the Post Office as a clerk and with fellow Corkonian Sam Maguire founded a unit of the I.R.A., using Post Office rifles for arms–drill, rifles stored in the event of a German invasion. Constance Gore–Booth, as befitting her lineage, was presented at Court as a débutante and was escorted in London Society by young army subalterns upon whom later she was to pull, literally, a blazing revolver in Dublin.

In Britain the ripples of the Gaelic Revival touched settled families of Irish descent, notably in Liverpool, Edinburgh, and Glasgow. Two of such lineal immigrant descent were James Connolly and Jim Larkin, both of whom spent formative years among the ghetto communities, were touched by the Gaelic Revival, went 'home' to Ireland and were subsequently to become powerful influences upon the Revolution of 1916. James Connolly founded the Citizen Army, probably the first 'people's militia' in these islands, consisting mainly of trade unionists and workers with a specific anti-capitalist bias which, while eschewing nationalism, was nonetheless drawn into active service in the Rebellion of 1916. His cohort from among the Irish in Britain, Jim Larkin, founded a trade union and both came to be regarded as the creative conscience of developing left–wing Labour philosophy in Ireland. Subsequently influential in their own particular way were Constance Gore–Booth, Douglas Hyde, the poet Yeats, and the future guerilla–leader Michael Collins. All were part of the London–Irish at the turn of the century.

Rarely has an émigré community welded together such disparate elements and formed in exile the future military, political and cultural leaders of a new state. The unifying link was the ethos of the Gaelic Revival, which began as the cultural dalliance of the socially privileged, sounded echoes among the depressed lower-middle classes in Ireland, and immigrant families in Britain; reverberated in the tolling of racial recall among the peasantry; and finally unleashed the potent force of Irish nationalism which gave birth to the Irish Republic in 1916.

If the lives of these luminaries among the immigrants in the early 1900s were irretrievably bound up with the Gaelic Revival, the lives of the majority of the immigrants were, as usual, not so diverted. For the majority, the day–to–day demands of ordinary experience were more important than the abstractions of nationalistic endeavour. It is true they were affected by the revival of nationalism, but in a cursory manner as a conversational topic for the majority, or perhaps attendance at an Irish Language class for a tiny minority. For most, the improvement of their social and economic lot was the prime consideration. Whereas the peak years of nineteenth-century emigration to Britain had been occasioned by the Great Famine and its aftermath, now at the beginning of the twentieth century, the settled pattern of immigration had economic and social roots; higher wages and better opportunities for individual improvement were the criteria of arrival in Britain. Wages, social conditions, educational opportunities for their children were what mattered more than the idealistic concepts of the Gaelic Ireland of the nationalists. The anti–Irish hostility of the immediate post–Famine decades had substantially diminished by the early 1900s; as mentioned earlier, the 'Oirish' had become an accepted part of working–class communities, and the Irish in turn accepted and thrived on the changed degree of acceptance. The advent of the First World War, with Britain rallying regiments to the defence of the 'small nations' provided a conflicting pull and was to set a choice of loyalties before the Irish in Britain. Overwhelmingly, they cast their loyalty for Britain. The decision of the Irish political leader, Redmond, that conscription should not be resisted, in return for promised Home Rule, led 200,000 Irishmen into the trenches of the Great War. Among the Irish in Britain, battalions were raised in Glasgow, Edinburgh, London, and Tyneside. From London the regiments of the Irish Guards and the London–Irish Rifles drew heavily on first and second generation Irish, thereby consolidating the tradition of émigré service in the British Army. The majority of the immigrants decided the 'freedom of the small nations' to be of more immediate import than the distant possible freedom of a more intimate 'small nation', an attitude cogently expressed in the following account of the charge of the London–Irish at Loos. The account, published in the *Weekly Dispatch* of October 1915, was written in hospital by an anonymous survivor of that slaughter of trench-warfare. Reading it now, one is struck by the immense depth of loyalty of many Irish towards Britain – and by the curious suppression of Anglo-Irish differences, as if that traditional quarrel was merely a family difference to be resolved by an outside threat: in this case from Germany.

Equally, the suspicion occurs that Irish soldiery were so valued by the British authorities that the extensive account was published with an eye to its recruiting powers – a suspicion reinforced by the introduction to the narrative which notes that '... it is of peculiar interest at a moment when a special appeal is being made for 500 more recruits for the regiment.'

Here is an extract from the account in the *Weekly Dispatch* mentioned above.

HOW THE LONDON IRISH SAVED AN ARMY CORPS

New Regiment's Glorious Rush and Stand at Battle of Loos

FOOTBALL DRIBBLED INTO ENEMY TRENCH

We were all kinds and creeds and parties in the regiment, and we often thought how only a little over a year ago we were on the point of civil war. But this war has taught us the oneness of the Empire; so you saw landlord and peasant, Catholic and Protestant, Unionist and Nationalist, all friendly as probably never before in Irish history, and all vowing vengeance on the Hun.

NOW THE TIME HAD COME!

As soon as we heard the great bombardment start we knew the big advance was going to begin; and for nineteen solid days the guns banged away, till, as one wit in the regiment put it, 'It was a wonder the shells didn't bally well jam together in the air,' so thick did they come over our heads. When we were ordered one night to the back reserve trenches and 'fed up well' we knew the time was near. 'Fattening the calf for slaughter,' said we to ourselves.

Then everyone began to settle his affairs in case the worst should happen – which is always done. Pals were arranging together that the survivor should write to the other's people and others were making their wills, and all that. There are lots of gentlemen rankers with us – one ranker, for example, when asked why he had made no separation allowance to his wife, simply replied that he had already made over £3,000 a year to her. I don't know what his name was. The cousin of the Earl of Donoughmore and the nephew of Lord Dunleath both used to be in the ranks.

I can't tell you the pride we felt when we heard that we were actually to have the honour of heading the division. Our first objective was to be Valley Cross Roads which commanded the way to Lees and Hill 70, after taking which we were, if possible, to break through as far as Lens, the key to Douain. After three days' good food and rest we were marched into the first trenches late at night, laden with ammunition, kitbags, and trench tools, and, in fact, everything we could carry.

THE GENERAL'S 'SEND-OFF'

Our first job was to get over the parapet and start digging about three hundred yards nearer to the enemy, and by dawn we had managed to make a sort of ditch about three foot deep all along our front. It was not dangerous work the first night, for the Germans had not spotted us, and we left off at dawn; but when they did spot the new earthworks and realized what we were up to, the first thing they did in the morning was to start a terrific bombardment. We had to lie low all day till it was safe enough to go out again under cover of darkness and complete the job – for we were told we should have to stay in them the next day.

I shall never forget that night. As we 'marched into battle', to use the old expression, the general – God bless him – took the officers one after the other by the hand, with a genial, 'Put it there, lad,' and 'Good luck,' and then said a few words to the men which stirred us to our inmost souls.

'The Empire expects great things of the London-Irish today – remember that – for you have been chosen to lead the whole division.' But, Heavens, you've got to be a soldier, and to have been under fire and facing death for weeks to be able to understand what such words mean. No man can hear them and remain a coward, for you just feel that all the old people at home would scorn to receive you back unless you had done your utmost.

A few minutes later we were crawling out into the open to finish the trench which was to be the springing-off place for the great dash that we hoped would break the German lines. No sooner had we reached this place than the stillness was broken by the roar of the enemy's guns, and bullets and shells poured on us, the explosions silhouetting us momentarily every few instants, and revealing us hard at work. How the beggars got the range I can't tell, they must have got it during the day, but it was deadly accurate, and they picked the men off continually.

Far from frightening us off the job, though, the only result was that it made us dig the harder for cover, and we got the trench five, and in some places six, feet deep. All the time – and it is as fine a thing as I've heard of during the war – our colonel and our officers, down to the youngest subaltern, walked calmly up and down in the open cheering us with words of encouragement and occasionally a drop from their own flasks. In fact, they were ready to do anything for us except to give us permission to smoke, and we knew that would have meant sentencing us to death.

Just before the order to charge we gave the enemy a touch of their own little game – gas. It was the first time we had used it – though God knows how we had clamoured for it ever since the terrible fate of the Canadians at Givenchy. We all got our own respirators on in case of a back wind, but the breeze was quite favourable, and suddenly great waves as white as cotton wool rolled over towards the enemy while our guns banged away over our heads like ten thousand thunderstorms. Yet even this was not loud enough to drown the cheers that went up from our own chaps. After the waves of gas another and, I think, a new device was used – namely, blinding smoke that went rolling off in the same way. It was followed by yet other waves of gas, and so on till the whole intervening space was filled. The last wave was a smoke wave; this was in order to enable our chaps to cover the distance between the two trenches under cover of its density.

All the while we had been holding ourselves ready to spring away like dogs upon a leash, and you could see right down the trench the chaps tightening a buckle here and a strap there. Everybody was in the best of spirits – in fact, I don't think we had ever felt keener for the fray. It seemed as if at last the war for us had really begun. Some looked a trifle pale, others were extra jolly, but all had a look of determination different from any expression they usually wore.

One set of our men – footballers by profession – made a strange resolution; it was to take a football along with them. The officer discovered this, and ordered the football to be taken back to the base – which, of course, was carried out. But the old members of the London Irish Football Club were not to be done out of the greatest game of their lives – the last to some of them, poor fellows – and just before Major Beresford gave the signal the leather turned up again mysteriously.

'ON THE BALL, LONDON IRISH!'

Suddenly the officer in command gave the signal, 'Over you go, lads.' With that the whole line sprang up as one man, some with a prayer, not a few making the sign of the cross. But the footballers, they chucked the ball over and went after it just as cool as if on the field, passing it from one to the other, though the bullets were flying thick as hail, crying, 'On the ball, London Irish,' just as they might have done at Forest Hill. I believe that they actually kicked it right into the enemy's trench with the cry, 'Goal!' though not before some of them had been picked off on the way.

There wasn't four hundred yards between the trenches and we had to get across the open – a manoeuvre we started just as on parade. All lined up with rifles at the slope. Once our fellows got going it was hard to get them to stop, with the result that some rushed clean into one of our own gas waves and dropped in it just before it had time to get over the enemy's trench.

The barbed wire had been broken into smithereens by our shells so that we could get right through – but we could see it had been terrible stuff, and we all felt we should not have had a ghost of a chance of getting through had it not been for an unlimited supply of shells expended on it.

No one can describe a charge. It's impossible. You can only feel it. Every step you take is a miracle of pluck, for all the time you can hear and see the stabs of steel and lead rushing past you. Just imagine trying to run down Oxford Street alone, with people at every window pelting half a dozen bricks at you. But it is impossible to describe – I give it up. The thing that struck me most, though, wasn't the danger: it was the voice of our dear old chaplain – the Padre, who actually made the charge with us – giving his blessing and absolution to the men as they fell on every side. God bless him!

When we reached the German trench, which we did under a cloud of smoke, we found nothing but a pack of beings dazed with terror. In a jiffy we were over their parapet and the real

work began; a kind of madness comes over you as you stab
with your bayonet and hear the shriek of the poor devil suddenly
cease as the steel goes through him and you know he's 'Gone
West'. The beggars did not show much fight, most having retired
into their second line of trenches when we began to occupy
their first to make it our new line of attack. That meant clearing
out even the smallest nook or corner that was large enough to
hold a man.

THE HAND-TO-HAND FIGHT

This fell to the bombers. Every bomber is a hero, I think,
for he has to rush on fully exposed, laden with enough stuff to
send him to 'kingdom come' if a chance shot or a stumble sets
him off.

Some of the sights were awful in the hand-to-hand struggle
– for, of course, that is the worst part. Our own second in
command, Major Beresford, was badly wounded. One officer
named Hamilton, though shot through the knee just after leaving
our trench, was discovered still limping on at the second German
trench and had to be placed under arrest to prevent his going
on till he bled to death. I saw a poor old sergeant burnt to
death by a petrol bomb which caught him in full in his chest. It
was the most terrible sight I ever saw in my life as he struggled
with the flames as they licked his face, screaming all the while
till he suddenly went raving mad with pain and dropped to the
ground like a log.

They got the worst of it, though, when it came to cold steel,
which they can't stand and they ran like hares. So having left
a number of our men in the first trench we went on to the
second and then the third, after which other regiments came
up to our relief and together we took Loos. It wasn't really our
job at all to take Loos, but we were swept on by the enthusiasm,
I suppose, and all day long we were at it, clearing house after
house, or rather what was left of the houses – stabbing and
shooting and bombing till one felt ready to drop dead one's
self. We wiped the 23rd Silesian Regiment right out, but it
was horrible to work on with the cries of the wounded going up
all round.

You have no idea how the place was fortified; sandbagged

up to the roof some of the houses were, with wonderfully concealed Maxims that could shoot so that you would not even see the flash from the muzzle.

As to their snipers, they are wonderfully plucky chaps, I must say; for some of them are a couple of hundred yards out ahead of their trenches buried up to the neck in a hole and with nothing but a fixed rifle with telescopic sight and an unlimited supply of food and ammunition, firing away till picked off themselves.

VAULTS GIVE UP − THE LIVING

The most ghastly part of the whole fight I think was the struggle in the cemetery. It had been practically turned into a fort, with great tombstones placed one on top of the other like sandbags, and wreaths and ornaments in pieces all around, and here and there like specks monuments and broken crosses and pillars. It was ghastly, death fighting death, so to speak; but we all realized there was no help for it − for the Germans had taken up the position thinking no doubt that the very sanctity of the place would protect them.

It simply went through you to see our guns aimed at the great white crosses and the splinters and stones flying in all directions; but this was nothing to the sights when the hand-to-hand fight began and we had to bayonet some of them on the very stones. As they came out of the vaults in which they had been hiding, it seemed for all the world as if the living could not supply sufficient food for the slaughter and the dead were rising again to die once more. A painter might have made it a picture of the Last Judgment for all the horror it contained.

It was the key to the position, however, and there was no room for sentiment. We remembered the words of the general − we were leading a division, and that was enough. We not only cleared the cemetery but went beyond it.

There seemed to be some mystery about Hill 70 − as to whether it was taken or not. As a matter of fact, Hill 70 is some five or six miles across; it is not a sort of Spion Kop. It is quite possible for the Germans and the English to be occupying it simultaneously without even realizing they were on a hill at all, so flat it is.

Now what really happened was this; our men went clean over it in the first rush that carried them beyond Loos in the direction of Lens, which we had hoped to capture. Unfortunately the Germans suddenly brought up tremendous reinforcements as soon as they realized that the loss of Lens would probably mean the loss of Douain, and concentrated their whole counter-attack upon some fresh troops who had only been out at the front a fortnight, and these, unused to the tricks that you learn after you've been under fire a few times, got into a disadvantageous position which at one moment nearly lost us all our gains.

THE GRIM STRUGGLE

Luckily during the advance a large quantity of supplies had been moved up from our old trenches to our new trenches, which were nothing more than the Germans' third line of trenches turned round back to front, the sandbag parapets having been moved sack by sack on to the other side and consolidated, as well as time would allow.

The battle now became terrific. It seemed as if the whole of Krupps was being chucked at us wholesale, while our own artillery was peppering away just as hard from behind our backs. It seemed as if they'd pop our heads off at times between them. 'Stick to it, lads,' said one of our officers; 'everything depends upon your holding your position. If they once break the line——' He didn't have to finish; that was quite sufficient, and the words of the General came back: 'Remember you're Irish and the Empire expects great things of you.'

That was enough. If every man Jack of us had to go under we were determined to do so, but we wouldn't give in. 'Von Hindenburg is coming with half a million men,' shouted one German, as he advanced. 'Begorra, then, so much the worst for Von Hindenburg and his half million,' we shouted; and the fight went on.

The barbed wire had of course been blown to shreds for our own advance, so we could not have its protection now the

Germans returned; but as fast as the beggars came we poured the lead into their solid masses till the very rifles burnt our hands and seemed every minute as if they would turn red hot.

There we were, a long way from our own lines; in fact, nearly in the enemy's, isolated from every help and hardly knowing what was happening around us or what part we were really playing in the great struggle. The strain on the nerves was something terrific; every moment you felt as if you were ready to drop from sheer exhaustion, but still you kept up, you couldn't tell yourself how. Every now and again your next pal would drop beside you with a scream, pipped in the head by a bullet, or in the body by a piece of shrapnel, and you dared not leave your post or lower your rifle a second for fear the great human wave that had to be shattered before it reached you would break over your parapet.

Some of them would be quite silent, but you could see their lips moving in prayer as they lay there; their thoughts no doubt far away among the green hills of old Ireland. Others you could feel writhing in agony and calling, 'Mother, mother, mother,' till you could feel the hot tears welling up in your own eyes, as you thought, especially if he happened to be a special pal, that the next day you would have to write to his people and tell the news as gently as possible. The night came on, but you knew you could not expect relief for hours – and you saw the dawn and wondered what fate it heralded for you.

There is nothing on earth more stupendous than dawn on a battlefield; the cold breeze, the streak of light, the rolling clouds, and the haze of night gradually lifting, but pierced here and there with the flash of rifle and Maxim gun, and the whole atmosphere shedding a kind of greenish colour on all the faces around. And all the while the thought is ever before your mind that any minute may be your last, and that the sun you see rise – you may never see set.

All Monday passed and still no relief came; indeed, it was a question whether any minute we should not be blown to atoms and the line swamped with a rush from the enemy. We could hardly stand from fatigue, having been in action steadily since Saturday morning; but still we fought on almost blindly.

'Fight on, lads,' said an officer who was afterwards killed,

poor chap. 'Remember the division looks to you. This is bound
to end sooner or later. Let it be in a way that will never be
forgotten when they hear of it at home in London and Ireland.'
So we fought on, and never a single German got nearer than
a dozen yards from our lines.

Soon we got the word that we should be relieved early
Tuesday morning under cover of the darkness. The announce-
ment sent a terrific thrill of joy through us, for then we knew
we had won.

VICTORY!

The last few hours, however, were terrific. Our own shells
had come to our rescue and under their shelter new troops came
to relieve us, together with the stretcher-bearers for our
wounded. As soon as we got to the back trenches in safety a
huge cheer went up from all the others. 'The London Irish –
Hurroo!' and they shook us by the hands and took our rifles
from our grasp and the kits from our backs in their eagerness
to show their gratitude.

One German prisoner whom we had brought in the day
before, however, scowled as he recognized us.

'Irish butchers,' he hissed in perfectly good English, to which
one of our chaps replied, 'Worse than you were in Belgium,
were we?' and the chap was silent.

The first few moments after battle are very wonderful, for
it is then that the rollcall takes place and you see for the first
time the terrible cost of victory. You hear pals calling out the
names of pals and no answer coming back, and then the poor
fellow who survives going round to get the last news. It's
terrible. You see chaps who have stood the strain of battle like
so many giants, now crying like children all alone.

'THE EMPIRE WILL BE PROUD'

Often and often you see a chap dropping on his knees and
thanking God aloud for his safety; and, though you might have
smiled in peace time, out there in war time you realize these
great truths, and – well, you follow suit. The chaplain, too – and

they are all bricks – comes round with a few words of the faith that has suddenly become so real and gives you his blessing.

Then you see others around full of the enthusiasm of the great hour, taking out their pencils and scraps of paper and cardboard or anything in order to let the people get the first news of their escape as quickly as possible and saying that everyone was telling how the 18th Battalion London Irish Regiment had saved the situation.

I put that down myself to the ordinary pride of regiment till we got it from the general himself, who assembled us together. 'Not only am I proud to have had the honour of being in command of such a regiment as yours, lads, but,' he said, 'the whole Empire will be proud whenever in after years the battle of Loos comes to be written; for I can tell you that it was the London Irish who helped to save a whole British army corps . . .'

*   *   *

With Irish logic, however, some who fought abroad for the Empire returned to Ireland, to take up arms against their former British Army colleagues and to participate in the Rebellion of 1916, declared on the ancient thesis that 'England's difficulty was Ireland's opportunity'. The Rebellion and subsequent Anglo–Irish War of 1917–21 proved heavily divisive among the Irish in Britain, most of whom now had some degree of loyalty to Britain and were bewildered by the Rebellion. Predictably, this division of loyalties was most severe in the traditional immigrant areas of the larger cities. In Glasgow, the immigrants' paper, the *Observer*, declared that the Rebellion was the 'madly criminal action of pro–German plotters'. Unswayed by such condemnation, units of the I.R.A. in Glasgow drilled and trained under the command of former British Army servicemen, using as handbook the Army training manual; men and women from the city went to Ireland to involve themselves in the Rebellion and its aftermath of guerilla war, and guns and ammunition were transferred to Dublin in appropriate containers of coffins ostensibly holding returned remains of immigrants. By 1920, the I.R.A. register in Glasgow numbered 4,000 recruits and the financial contribution from among the Scottish communities was reckoned by De Valera to be in excess of funds from any other country, including Ireland.

From Liverpool and London travelled detachments of I.R.A. volunteers, to aid the Rebellion, reflecting a community divisiveness that was poignant and bizarre. After the fall of the rebel–held Post Office in Dublin, an Irish–born officer of a regiment but shortly landed, passed on O'Connell Bridge a detachment of rebel prisoners which included the officer's brother. The prisoners' uniform could well have been of a batch designed by the Irish editor of a leading London financial journal who, in response to a request from Republican friends in Dublin, had visited some military tailors in London and selected items of design from the officer uniforms of many countries' armies. The resulting composite formed the uniform of some of the rebel soldiers of the new Republic.

The London Irish saw the uniforms during the month of October 1920 when an I.R.A. detachment escorted the emaciated body of Terence McSwiney from Brixton Prison to Southwark Cathedral (built by the contribution of the immigrant poor) where it lay in state. McSwiney, Republican Lord Mayor of Cork, died after seventy-four days on hunger strike in protest against the activities of the Black and Tans in Ireland. His funeral procession was an emotive affair, but it is doubtful if more than a minority of the hundred thousand Irish who lined the London streets agreed with the sacrificial nature of his Republicanism or sympathized with his concept of the need for armed struggle. Not the least of their many conflicting reactions may have been the thought that, for most of them, the simple act of emigrant transference across the Irish Sea had brought the material and social benefits which McSwiney and his colleagues hoped their militant sacrifice would eventually bestow upon Ireland. Sadly, the post–Revolutionary Irish Government did not fulfil the ideals of vastly improved living standards and opportunities. In the 1920s, of course, such disillusion harboured in the distant future, and the immigrants were sufficiently sceptical of miracles being wrought. Accordingly they paid easy lip service to the idea of an Ireland free of British Rule, while determining that their own interests might best be served by remaining in Britain. Even the subsequent ratification of an Irish Free State incurred no great rushing 'home' from among the 750,000 Irish–born in Britain.

Rather were the immigrants determinedly consolidating their claim upon Britain, becoming involved at many levels of indigenous life. Socially, they formed a weighty rump of the working classes, politically they supported the growing Labour party and in the inherited tradition of Feargus O'Connor's radicalism, the newly–formed Communist party of Great Britain in 1920 numbered three of Irish descent[11] among its founders. In the traditionally radically–orientated communities of Lancashire they were prominent in the growth of trade unions and nationwide they formed the backbone of Roman Catholic religious expansion. They had, indeed, little to complain of in their absorption into the passive mainstream of British life.

There were, of course, repercussions from the native population arising from the viscissitudes of the war in Ireland and the reactions to charge and counter–charge of brutality which emanated in newspaper reports from Ireland. When, in November 1920, the execution 'squad' of the former Kensington Post Office clerk, Michael Collins (now Commander of the anti–British guerilla forces) shot fourteen British army officers in Dublin, the interiors of several 'Irish' public houses in working-class districts of London were smashed up by infuriated Cockney mobs. There were also some attempts to damage Catholic churches. Members of the I.R.A. in Britain later 'retaliated' by firing warehouses on Tyneside and smashing shop windows in London's Oxford Street, but the mass of the immigrants remained but little affected by the bloody bitterness of the war; many of them, anyway, had seen sufficient of war's destruction in the service of the Empire. But even within the ranks of Irishmen still serving in the Army, divisions were made manifest. One such manifestation centred around the figure of Michael Collins who had spent ten formative years within the ranks of the London–Irish, where he had frequented Gaelic League meetings and played hurling with the Geraldines G.A.A. club in London.

Having headed an I.R.A. guerilla campaign in Ireland which brought the political leaders of the two nations to the conference table, Michael Collins arrived in London as part of the Irish negotiating team which faced, among others, the British Premier Lloyd George and the young Winston Churchill. He held the rank of Commander–in–Chief of the I.R.A. and tumultuous crowds of the London–Irish turned out to 'welcome him back'; among those with whom he renewed acquaintance was his sister, Johanna Collins, who had calmly stayed at her London desk in the Civil Service while her brother had returned to wage war on the British administration in Ireland.

The conference was marked by a formal cessation of hostilities in Ireland to encourage as calm as possible an atmosphere. But the calm was very nearly shattered by the individualistic action of a sergeant of the Irish Guards regiment – a regiment which had lost almost 2,500 men and acquired four Victoria Crosses in the war ended two years previously. As the result of an inebriated reaction to the negotiations, Sergeant Roche and two I.R.A. men made off with arms from the regimental depot at Royal Windsor. They were arrested, but the raid, and its I.R.A. implications, made almost intractable the already bitter negotiations (Michael Collins had no prior knowledge of the seizure of arms). It was through the diplomacy of another London–Irish personality, the painter John Lavery, that some hurried measure of accommodation was restored. John Lavery knew Winston Churchill—whom he was later to tutor in painting—and it was over a comparatively relaxed evening at the painter's dinner table that some meagre measure of entente was restored.

The Treaty finally negotiated and ratified by both Parliaments consigned approximately three–quarters of the island of Ireland to freedom from British Sovereignty. The remaining quarter or so of Ulster was to become—and currently is— the subject of bitter dispute. The Irish in Britain were to remain for the most part unaffected by the subsequent course of that dispute, although one of the most immediate effects of the Anglo–Irish Treaty was to influence the international legal status of successive generations of immigrants to Britain.

Emigrants leaving Ireland after 1922 could then, for the first time, legally regard themselves as Irish. The international legal recognition of Irish Citizenship came into being – though the 'benefits' of that status must have been questioned by the Irish who came in ever–increasing numbers to Britain in the years immediately following the Treaty. By 1925, they were entering Britain at a steady pace which reflected the incompetence of

the post–Revolutionary Irish Governments and provided, by
their emigration, ample evidence for those who held the views
that 'the Irish were incapable of governing themselves'. Even
with the effects of the Land Act of the previous year, which
divided up the former estates of absentee landlords, the
immigration of the Irish to Britain continued at a substantial
rate. Those who came were for the most part from rural areas
and followed the traditional occupations; the men in labouring
and navvying, the women in domestic service.

Effects of the British–sponsored educational improvements
were, however, to be perceived in the growth of what was
colloquially referred to as 'a better–educated class of immigrant',
in the influx of graduates of the Catholic University founded in
Dublin by the English Cardinal Newman. This increased influx
of graduates, mainly doctors and dentists, did not, however,
receive a welcome from the equivalent stratum of the host
society. Anti-Irish resentment occasioned by the Rebellion of
1916 – seen by many middle-class British as a 'stab in the
back' during the war with Germany – lingered well into the
twenties and was to some extent intensified by the Anglo-Irish
Treaty of 1921. Thus many of the Irish Catholic graduates
who came to Britain in the immediate post-Treaty years were
regarded as disloyal Sinn Feiners who now had the temerity
to seek professional positions in a country whose sovereignty
over Ireland had been rejected. Many Irish graduates found
themselves unwelcome in the London clubs which catered for
the professions – and they reacted by forming a separate club
for Irish graduates in Britain. The *Observer* of 14 December
1928 carried this notice:

National University of Ireland Dining Club

It is proposed to establish in London a
Dining Club for graduates of the National
University of Ireland. If any of your
readers who are graduates of the University
would like to have some further information, and write to me, I shall be pleased to
correspond with them.

T. J. Kiernan

The notice was also reproduced in the weekly Catholic papers. From the response was founded the National University of Ireland Club, initially with premises near Westminster Cathedral, later to become a favourite location of Irish middle-class clubs and societies. Following the severe class prejudices of the time, the graduates formed a self–congratulatory ghetto, separated from the Irish working–class ghettos, not by either accent or temperament, but rather by would–be social status. The graduates were understandably sensitive as to their precise social status in a society which functioned rigidly on such distinctions; this writer was told of the indignant reaction of one medical member of the N.U.I. Club on finding his Irish maid present in the club one evening, on the arm of a fellow-member. Such embarrassment... and the possibility that the innocent girl might be tempted to become familiar on the morrow, in front of the medical member's English patients!

Such were the pressures of the late 1920s for the 'better-educated class of immigrant' who came in increasing propor-tions, sensitive to the stock judgements of a society which saw all 'Oirish' immigrants in the cast of Punch cartoon characters.

We can imagine the effects upon the medical member of the University Club, had he purchased in London's Charing Cross Road 'a book for children' of the 1920s, which contained this verse:

> The Irish Child can dance a jig
> And share its pillow with a pig
> And where we ask for pie or meat
> The praties he is glad to eat.

That graduates and others would seek to separate themselves from the mass of working–class immigrants is understandable, but the divisions, nevertheless, mitigated against any efforts to alleviate the depressed state of the mass of immigrants – the graduate body could be held to be the natural leaders of the immigrant community. Had they been able to overcome the separatist social pressures of the host society, it is fair to say that inroads could have been made upon these 'social problems' of drunkenness, unemployment, lack of vocational direction

which characterized a substantial minority of their working–
class compatriots, making them figure disproportionately in
criminal and health statistics: in the 1930s the contribution
from among the immigrant Irish to the total prison population
did not fall below 20 per cent when they hardly numbered
2 per cent of the population. Native newspapers were not
reticent in identifying the nationality of those who appeared
before the courts or who formed a substantial proportion of
those treated for tuberculosis in British hospitals. The
Famine imagery still sounded echoes and some of the tensions
of that era were revived with the Depression of the early 1930s.

This lack of community leadership was the greatest single
deficiency which the immigrants suffered. The homeland of the
time, by contrast, began to formulate progressive economic and
social measures, albeit in the face of meagre human and financial
resources and with the burden of an inexperienced administra–
tion at a time when, as Sean O'Faolain has recorded, 'the
Catholic Church was felt, feared and courted on all sides as
the dominant power', with attendant inhibiting effects upon
progressive social policies. For the Irish workers in Britain there
was a profound absence of social leadership, rendering them as
mere factory and building–site fodder, totally at the whim of
economic forces. Only in the traditional immigrant areas of
Scotland and the North–East was there in existence the sem–
blance of a receiving community structure into which they
could absorb with confidence, being the continuum of previous
generations' activity in community and trade union affairs.

1930s

Accordingly, it was in these areas, notably Liverpool, New–
castle, Rochdale, and Leeds that many rural Irish began to
consolidate their claim upon the host country, against a back–
ground of Depression fears of the thirties. In this they were
aided by the trenchant friendship of the descendants of previous
generations of immigrants who were strong in the local Catholic
and working–class communities. In other areas, by comparison,
there was little encouragement to settle; it was not uncommon,
for instance, for factories in the Coventry and Birmingham
regions to display 'No Irish need apply' signs alongside notice–

boards of vacancies. Similar declarations were prominent on accommodation notice–boards in parts of Scotland with the added rider of 'No Catholics'. One can only hazard at the mixed feelings of the Irish Protestant immigrants—who formed a steady trickle of the overall immigration—to such notices.

Hardly surprising then that the Irish conformed to the previous century's pattern of seeking shelter in the most run–down and dilapidated districts; the men sleeping two to a bed in overcrowded rooms, for which privilege they paid £1 a week in 1938, when the average industrial weekly wage was £5.

There was more private, if rudimentary, accommodation in Camden Town's Rowton House, a hostel barracks of the Railway Age, which still stands as a monument to the eternal verities of immigration. Patrick Kavanagh, the poet of bitter, barren, rural Ireland, stayed there for a time during his 'literary emigration' to London in 1935, and afterwards wrote that: 'many Irish boys made Rowton House, Camden Town, first stop from Mayo. The soft voices of Mayo and Galway sounding in that gaunt, impersonal place fell like warm rain on the arid patches of my imagination.' His compatriots in Rowton House, Kavanagh judged to be 'true peasants. They walked with an awkward gait and were shy. To me they looked up as to a learned man and posed me crooked questions which I couldn't answer.... I had seen too much of them in Ireland. Their characters, impressionable as wax, were soon to wear the impress of common vulgarity.' The poet did not take to London; his heart lay in the rejected rural reaches, and with pastoral imagery he perhaps articulated the feelings of his 'true peasants' when he wrote:

'London is a pagan city and it is not the poetic paganism of blackbirds. After the chaste paganism of Ireland, London's materialist immorality terrified me. . . . There was little innocent courting; on Hampstead Heath I saw them copulating like dogs in the sun. . . . I returned to Ireland. Ireland green and chaste and foolish. And when I wandered over my materialist immorality terrified me. . . . There was little of this life and I saw that it was good.'

For most of the inhabitants of Rowton House there was no such happy return to Ireland 'green and chaste' but rather the immigrant grind ahead. Their social gathering places were, predictably, the public houses, and then they felt most at ease only in the most scruffy of these premises. As an immigrant 'community' of labourers, porters and navvies they felt as put–upon and as subject to native resentment as their antecedents of the Famine diaspora. They suffered profoundly, as has been mentioned, from the lack of concern from among their better–off countrymen. One veteran of the thirties, now a prosperous building contractor in London, recalled for me the severity of divisions between the working–class Irish and 'professional' Irish.

'There was simply no meaningful contact. We stuck to our circuit and they stuck to theirs. Occasionally, we might meet an Irish architect or doctor at some Church function, but they always struck me as being embarrassed when we met and when I told them I was a carpenter . . . though we both had our best suits on and no doubt could have had a lot in common to talk about . . . but I sensed their tightness, somehow. Mind you, I was from Mayo, and these people would be from a city such as Dublin or Cork. Perhaps, looking back on it, I was extra–sensitive myself, country people always are, you know. We think the "city slicker" is looking down on us. I remember at dances now, I'd take a girl up that might be from my part of the country and I'd say "where are you from?" and she'd put on this awfully, you know, accent and say, "I'm from Dublin, *actually*". And she'd probably be a maid or waitress . . . or something like that.

'Mind you, we were all very sensitive and unsure then. We'd cling together a lot with lads from our own county. After Mass we'd go to a pub in Leeds frequented by Mayo men. The talk would be mostly about Mayo and who was doing what back there – or about Mayo men here, and what they were doing in the "diggin's". After that we might have a meal, but never in a place that looked "proper", with tablecloths and so on. We'd be scared to go into a place like that, even on Sunday with our best suits on, in case they'd throw us out for not knowing how to behave properly at table. We all shared rooms in digs, and sometimes we shared beds—but no immorality mind you—and sent money home most weeks and said we were getting on fine at the buildin'—even though in the thirties we'd have work only about three weeks out of four. When you met someone you knew, the remark always was "Are ye workin'?" It was up to yourself to get work when it was scarce, by letting on to a foreman what a great worker you could be if you were given a job. Some fellows used to develop a particular way of walking, coming onto a site to look for work —they called it "The Gimp"—it amounted to a sort of swagger which gave an impression of confidence. When a fellow with "The Gimp" came onto a site, he'd kick any ould timber outa his way—fuck it outa his way, as much as to say: "You want a tunnel dug . . . I'll dig it myself in a day. . . ."

'And then coming to England with the lads and sticking together, being afraid to talk to the English girls, and all the time this brooding thing of history . . . well, it didn't help you know in so-called integrating. I was fifteen years here before I came to know English people properly—and that only happened when I started up my own business, and met them as an equal, in a manner of speaking. Now, I'll tell you something. I'd prefer to do business with an Englishman any day of the week; they're more honest than the Irish and they keep their discretion as well as their delivery dates. And they don't have the malice the Irish have towards each other, resenting the fellow that gets on in the world . . . resenting the fellow who pulls himself up out of the spite.

'Sometimes now I go for a stroll around Camden Town, after Mass on a Sunday, and the lads are still there, just like I was in Leeds all them years ago, only now they're in Greek and Eyetalian cafes, having their Sunday grub, because they're not wanted in the digs. I look at them, all atin' away without a word between them, stuffin' mixed grills down their gollops . . . and I'm glad them days are behind me.

'You ask me if there was any Community help? Ah, you're jokin' using phrases like that. What Community? We relied on ourselves. We felt we were only tolerated by the English, by landladies and such . . . and by employers because we were good at digging. Sometimes, if we were feeling belligerent, which usually followed on feeling miserable, we'd go to an "English" pub, waiting to hear some crack about "the Paddies" or "the Micks" – looking for an excuse to start a barney, you know.

'Looking back on it now, thirty years afterwards, I can see what was wrong with us. Now that I've had a bit of time to read and think about these things, I can see we were too wrapped up in ourselves. In a way we suffered from two things: coming from rural Ireland and from the education we had there. In the country, you see, we hardly ever met English people, and our Christian Brother[13] education was very anti-British . . . The Black and Tans and 1920 and all that sort of thing.

'It was a case of every man for himself during the week, and then the pub on Sunday where you could pretend to be friends again.

'I'll tell you one thing though. It made us look out for ourselves, made us self-reliant.'

Apart from the efforts of some individual priests, the only concerted effort to combat the 'hard times' of the thirties appears to have come from the Connolly Association in London, which in 1935 produced the paper, *Irish Freedom** which urged its readers to join trade unions and to absorb the heady philosophy of the socialist James Connolly, executed for his part in the 1916 Rebellion. It was also watchful of instances of discrimination against Irish workers, without having much resources to combat such acts beyond publicizing the circumstances of such cases.

The founders of the Connolly Association toured Britain in pursuit of their efforts to politicize immigrant workers towards left–wing socialism, tirelessly banging their political heads on two brick walls of ingrained cultural resistance: the innate caution of most Irish workers and the antagonism of Irish priests, who often warned from the pulpit against the Connolly Association. (One of the Association's founders, Desmond Greaves, in fact personally encouraged his followers to attend their religious services.)

* Later re-named the *Irish Democrat*.

By 1938, with the advent of war with Germany but a year away, more militant demands were being made upon some of the immigrants to join the I.R.A., with the promise of 'action' in Britain when hostilities with Germany began. But that organization made even less headway than the Connolly Association among the immigrants. Most of the I.R.A. 'bombers' who waged the subsequent cruel Bombing Camgaign upon the civilian population came over specifically from Ireland to do so; the mass of the immigrants, however, did not see much point in abusing the hospitality of their hosts. In spite of their disavowel of such activities, the Bombing Campaign nevertheless affected their shaky relationship with the host community, as did the Republic's policy of neutrality during the war. It is worth briefly tracing these twin developments in relation to the Irish in Britain.

THE I.R.A. BOMBING CAMPAIGN sprang directly from the Anglo–Irish Treaty of 1921, which conceded, as we have seen, self–determination to twenty–six of Ireland's thirty–two counties. The remaining six (sometimes referred to as Ulster) because of the inherited militant loyalty to Britain of the majority of its inhabitants (descendants of Scots–Protestant Planters since the sixteenth century), remained within the United Kingdom. The Treaty, though ratified by the Irish Parliament (The Dail) resulted in Civil War in Southern Ireland between the factions prepared to settle for a twenty-six County Republic and the diehards who would settle for nothing less than a thirty-two County Republic.

Through the twenties and thirties those who held fast to that ideal of a thirty–two County Republic engaged in sporadic military enterprise. The advent of Britain's war with Germany reactivated the I.R.A. to old campaigning. Three years before the outbreak of the Second World War, an I.R.A. leader on a visit to America declared the intention of waging a 'military' campaign on Britain, in the event of hostility between Britain and Germany. He was, in part, succumbing to Irish–American anti–British euphoria, a legacy bequeathed by Famine folklore to the New World: said the I.R.A. leader, Sean Russell: (1) When hostilities start we shall certainly send 'planes to bomb England. (2) We also have quantities of ammunition and other war materials in England. (3) In England ... we have another secret army of Irishmen who meet quietly for drill and target practice.

Comment on the actual reality behind these claims is salutary, for it illustrates the mixture of naivety and self-deception which led to the Bombing Campaign: (1) The I.R.A. had no 'planes. (2) The total armaments of the I.R.A. in Britain amounted to less than two dozen assorted firearms. (3) The 'secret army of Irishmen' amounted to less than a hundred ill–trained juveniles and adults out of a total Irish population of 850,000.

Nevertheless, the campaign got off to a fatal start and a Mancunian worker died when a sewer was blasted with a time–bomb. This was rapidly followed by a series of further explosions aimed against innocent civilians as home–made but lethal bombs went off in litter–bins, subway stations, and left–luggage booths at main line stations, maiming and crippling bystanders and passers–by. After fifty–four such attacks in London, the Government brought in the Prevention of Violence Bill in July 1939 which compelled Irishmen in Britain to register with the police – a lineal descendant of a Government order of four hundred years previously to contain the problem of Irish vagrants. The Special Branch and Scotland Yard made weekly arrests, aided by the amateurism of their prey. Many of the adolescents stored large quantities of potassium chlorate in their 'digs', and were duly given away by landladies. Others, purchasing 'alarum' clocks—which triggered the explosives of which potassium was part—were politely asked to wait by shop assistants who then telephoned the police. Who were the bombers, and what did they feel? For the most part they were young I.R.A. men, brought up in that narrow Republican Religion which laid the cause of all Ireland's ills at Britain's door. Many were adolescents, who took to the more adventurous zeal of Republicanism, at an age when many adolescents develop a zealous philosophy of some kind. (The depleted social and economic conditions of Ireland in the late thirties proved a fertile breeding–ground for the excesses of Republicanism.) One of these adolescents was the sixteen–year–old Brendan Behan, playwright–to–be, whose subsequent best–selling novel *Borstal Boy*, opens with an account of his arrest in Liverpool:

Friday, in the evening, the landlady shouted up the stairs: 'Oh God, oh Jesus, oh Sacred Heart. Boy, there's two gentlemen to see you.'

I knew by the screeches of her that these gentlemen were not calling to inquire after my health, or to know if I'd had a good trip. I grabbed my suitcase, containing Pot. Chlor, Sulph Ac, gelignite, detonators, electrical and ignition, and the rest of my Sinn Fein conjuror's outfit, and carried it to the window. Then the gentlemen arrived.

A young one, with a blond, Herrenvolk head and a B.B.C. accent shouted, 'I say, greb him, the bestud'.

When I was safely grabbed, the blond one gave me several punches in the face, though not very damaging ones. An older man, in heavy Lancashire speech, told him to leave me alone, and to stop making a —— of himself . . . There were now two or three others in the room, and this old man was the sergeant and in charge of the raid.

He took some Pot. Chlor and sugar out of the case, put it in the empty fireplace and lit it with a match. It roared into flame and filled the room with smoke. He nodded to me and I nodded back.

Saxonhead and another, a quiet fellow, had me gripped by the arms.

'Got a gun, Paddy?' asked the sergeant.

'If I'd have had a gun you wouldn't have come through that door so shagging easy.'

He looked at me and sighed, as if I had said nothing, or as if he had not heard me.

'Turn him over', he told the quiet one.

Blondie began to search me with violence.

'No, not you', said the sergeant, 'Vereker'.

Vereker searched me, quietly, and, even along the seams of my flies, with courtesy.

'Lift your arms up over your head. Put your leg up. Thank you.'

From an inside pocket he took my money, a forged travel

permit, and a letter which happened to be written in Irish.

It was from a boy in Dublin who was sick in bed and wanted me to come and see him. He was a dreary bastard in any language, and I, a good–natured and affectionate boy, found him distressing to meet and embarrassing to avoid. I would have a good excuse for not meeting him for some time to come.

The blonde studied the Gaelic writing over Vereker's shoulder.

Disgusted, he turned to me and shouted, 'You facquing bestud, how would you like to see a woman cut in two by a plate–glass window?'

I would have answered him on the same level – Bloody Sunday, when the Black and Tans attacked a football crowd in our street; the massacre at Cork; Balbriggan; Amritsar; the R.A.F. raids on Indian villages. I had them all off, and was expecting something like this. But the sergeant said in a reasonable tone:

'Well, Paddy, there are people gathered round this house, and I don't think they mean you any good.' He laughed a bit. 'But take no heed of them. We'll get you to the Assizes all right. Safe and sound.'

Vereker released my arm and went to the window. 'Uniformed men are making them move along.'

The sergeant told Blondie to let me go.

'We'll sit here a while', he said, sitting on the side of the bed, grunting. He pointed, and I came over and sat beside him.

'I wish to Christ I was your age, Paddy, I'd had something better to do than throwing bombs around. How old are you?'

'I'm sixteen, and I'll be seventeen in February.'

*   *   *

Behan's bombs did not, thankfully, go off: but he did, to Borstal. Liverpool was one city to witness immediate results of the campaign, with outbreaks of communal violence; Glasgow and Edinburgh saw similar inter–communal incidents as a result. The worst explosion occurred in Coventry in August 1939, a month before the outbreak of war when a bomb left in the carrier of a cycle in the main shopping thoroughfare of

Broadgate exploded with the loss of five lives and the maiming of another twelve. Among the dead was an eighty-two-year-old man, and in the nature of such tragedies, a girl of twenty-one, due to be married a fortnight hence. Two days later, I.R.A. prisoners in Dartmoor had to be hospitalized as the result of beatings by other inmates. Subsequently two Irishmen, Barnes and McCormick, were executed for the offence, but the man who actually planted the bomb escaped. As recently as 1970, listeners to the B.B.C. midday news programme heard that man in a recorded broadcast from Dublin, say feelingly: 'Ah, poor Barnes, poor Barnes, he was innocent, you know.'

Such indulgence in pathos—from the safety of Ireland—must have sounded unfeelingly brutal to English listeners. Certainly the campaign provoked outbreaks of hostility against the Irish in Britain, a hostility which survives today in sparse pockets. (In 1969 a feud in the Fulham area of London, between an Irish publican and some local villains erupted into shooting and maiming: the ill-feeling was compounded in part by the thirty-year-old memory of an I.R.A. explosive cache found in Fulham during the campaign. Fulham, an area of tightly-knit Cockney families, had been the object of repeated German bombing during the war.)

In the face of alienation of the British population, the bombing campaign lasted a year, involving around 200 explosions, the death and injury of civilians, the jailing of eighty Irishmen—some of whom never quite recovered from the incarceration—and the removal of tons of explosives from lodging houses in Irish districts of Manchester, London, Liverpool, Glasgow, and Birmingham. The effects upon the Irish in Britain were to linger well into the fifties. The immediate effect at the time was to question the 'loyalty' of the three-quarters of a million Irish who worked in Britain throughout the war effort, notably at civilian level in the munitions factories and in the construction of aerodromes, and at military level in the forces. The trustworthiness of the immigrant Irish was questioned by Winston Churchill at meetings of the war cabinet (at which Churchill probably had the advice of his Minister of Information, the Tipperary-born

Brendan Bracken, on the subject). The trustworthiness of the 150,000 Irishmen in the forces was not (as far as we know) raised by the Prime Minister who was later to praise 'the temper and instincts of the thousands of Irishmen who hastened to the battle–front to prove their ancient valour'.

The Bombing Campaign finally petered out in the lengthy jail sentences. Longer term effects upon the Irish community generally was that democratic tarring of all birds with the same brush, most starkly seen in the reluctance to promote Irish-born to supervisory or management positions in many areas of business for many years afterwards, so that many were held back from personal development and usefulness. An additional element was provided by the running verbal and diplomatic battle between Churchill and Irish Prime Minister De Valera throughout the war over the use of Southern Irish ports.

1940s: THE ISSUE OF PORTS AND NEUTRALITY

Stock questions posed by puzzled Britishers to their Irish friends throughout the war were: 'Why are you neutral?', and 'Why don't you let us use the Irish ports?' The issues lay, as do so many contemporary issues, in the Anglo–Irish Treaty of 1921; one of the provisions of that Treaty being that Britain continued to have strategic naval bases in the Irish Republic, notably on the south–western Irish coast which looked out onto the Atlantic shipping routes. By 1938, however, De Valera, possibly with an eye to impending hostilities, had negotiated the 'return' of the ports with the British Naval Secretary.

Churchill, on assuming leadership of the British war effort in 1939, was furious on discovering the *fait accompli* and took the view that the Government of Southern Ireland (Eire) had repudiated the Treaty of 1921 over the issue of the ports, in that the handing back had not been ratified by the West-minster Parliament. With the Republic's declaration of neutrality, and the necessity of keeping the shipping–lanes free from German harassment, the issue of the ports became critical.

The British population at large was bewildered by Ireland's policy of neutrality and angered by her refusal to grant British

Sea-routes from Ireland to Britain in the 1850s, and the passage of the '. . . teeming Irish who trekked off the boats, stunned and sick by the twelve-hour, open-deck crossing.'

How the Irish came to Britain . . .

From a community such as this one (photographed in Co. Donegal in the 1860s) came t
Irish to Britain in the great post-famine exodus.

Note the facial features of the men in the front row, providing detail for exaggeration i
the ape-like creature (*right*), the artist's excess having been inspired by the Fenian outrag

Railway navvies in the 185(

'For the Irish who took to navvying, the 10,000 miles which they helped build in the lat
1840s had a significant effect upon them. To begin with, they had to overcome the rese
ment of native navvies; for all the handed down myths that the Irish built the railwa
rarely did they exceed a third of the overall navvy force. Resentment against them w
strong, and pitched battles occurred between navvy groups of opposing nationalities . .

1850: Completion of the Britannia Tubular Bridge over the Menai Straits provided rail link from the Welsh ports to London, and helped Irish immigrants who had previously trekked from Liverpool, or along the Great West Road from the port of Bristol. Today, 120 years later, this rail route still carries the bulk of Irish into Britain.

1852: Stockport, near Manchester. Riots sparked off by an Irish-Catholic procession.
'... the mob then proceeded to treat the houses on Rock Row (*above*) in like manner, reducing them to complete wrecks and next demolished the interior of Edgeley Chapel ...' (*below*).

1867: Clerkenwell, London, after the Fenians had exploded a barrel of gunpowder in an attempt to rescue a prisoner.

'The prisoner survived the explosion of a barrel of gunpowder, but a row of houses were demolished and twelve occupants died.'

London. Funeral of Terence McSwiney.
1920: 'The London-Irish saw the uniforms at first hand during the month of October 1920, when an I.R.A. detachment escorted the emaciated body of Terence McSwiney from Brixton Prison to Southwark Cathedral (built by the contributions of the immigrant poor), where it lay in state.'

McSwiney's funeral procession through London.

Terence Joseph McSwiney

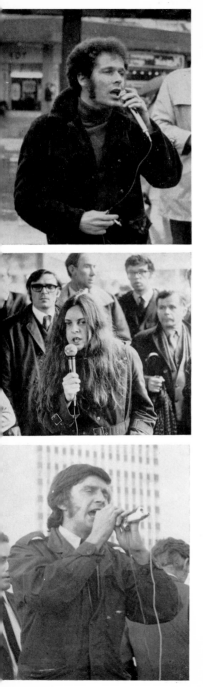

Eamonn McCann: 'There is no horde of proletarian Irish, enraged by Army brutality in Belfast, ready and waiting to pour out from Camden Town, Cricklewood and Kilburn to stop the heart of Empire ...'

Bernadette Devlin, M.P.

Gery Lawless of Irish Solidarity Campaign, organizers of a march in Glasgow in 1971 which resulted in communal violence.

'startled the Commons w
a spluttering of CS gas .
James Anthony Roche, on
release from Pentonville Pri
after serving sentence in co
nection with the CS gas in
dent in Parliament July 19

Brendan Magill, convicted
connection with an I.R
bomb-making class in Sov
London in 1970, and reput
to be the leader of the I.R.
in Britain at the time. '. . . h
lived a law-abiding life
Britain—until the trauma
his native Northern Irela
awoke a Republicanism t
was to land him in the dock

Hurling at London's Wembley stadium.

'Most Irish, however, tend to divest themselves of outward signs of Irishness. Only a minority support such traditional activities as the Gaelic games (*previous page*) or Irish dancing—photographed in a London Street (*above*).

Their children will grow up in a British society that is becoming increasingly multi-racial, characterized by these London children, cavorting for the camera in a Notting Hill playground.

access to the ports—anger heightened when the German U–boats began to take their deadly toll of shipping ferrying vital war supplies to Britain via the Atlantic artery. The North Atlantic, by contrast, was protected by the Shackleton aircraft which patrolled those routes from bases in Ulster. Writing to his Dominions Secretary, who dealt with Eire, Churchill in January 1941 said:

> No attempt should be made to conceal from Mr De Valera the depth and intensity of feeling against the policy of Irish neutrality ... should the present situation last until the end of the war ... a gulf will have opened between Northern and Southern Ireland which it will be impossible to bridge in this generation.

Even with the drastic fatalities which British ships incurred off the Irish coast, the Dublin Government stuck hard by its policy. On 21 March 1941, reacting to heavy losses of ships in the Atlantic, Churchill suggested to his First Lord of the Admiralty that radar installations (by then being rapidly developed) could be set up on Tory Island, off the Donegal coast, and possibly on some islands off the Kerry coast. His scheme to gain access to the islands was that they 'might be leased privately by some wealthy American friends'.

The British advanced developments of radar techniques may have had a side–effect upon Ireland's neutrality. After the year June 1940–June 1941, when Britain suffered over 43,381 dead and 50,856 wounded through bomb attacks, the British developed a radar system of deflecting the radio beams which German pilots used to guide them to British cities. An effect of the deflectionary technique was to direct enemy bombs away from inhabited areas and on to open country; which may have accounted for German bombs falling upon the Irish towns of Drogheda and Wicklow. This brought due apologies from the Axis Powers, but nevertheless tested the conviction of the Irish Government to remain neutral.

The Irish Government, though scrupulously maintaining the balance of official neutrality was, when the balance occasionally tilted, 'neutral in favour of Britain', not least in keeping

D

open the food routes to Britain and in the tacit encouragement throughout the war of the steady departure of emigrants to Britain facilitated by a U.K. permit office opened in Dublin. The office also directed the workers to specific areas as a condition of admission to Britain.

The permit office was administered with the co–operation of the Dublin Government and in the early years of war, emigrant batches of upwards of 2,000 a week were strategically directed to parts of Britain — hardly the act of a totally neutral Government. As a result of the earlier I.R.A. activity, all the Irish immigrants were required to register with the police and report any changes of address or occupation. Being wartime, all the labour force was strategically deployed; the Irish being assigned to harvest gathering, aerodrome construction, bombed–building demolition and munitions factories in the Midlands, the last location providing an ironic postscript to Churchill's displeasure at being denied the use of southern Irish ports. During the same month as he wrote stiff letters to his staff regarding the ports, the arms-factories in Small Heath, Birmingham—earlier the object of Churchill's pressing interest—increased their rifle production through the substantial addition of Irish immigrant labour. Neither was the Irish membership of the armed forces insignificant, a contribution duly acknowledged at the end of the war by Churchill, in his Victory broadcast of 13 May 1945, when he contrasted the attitude of the Irish Government with that of Irishmen who had fought in the war. Said Churchill:

We had only the North–Western approach between Ulster and Scotland through which to bring the means of life and to send out the forces of war. Owing to the action of the Dublin Government, so much at variance with the temper and instincts of thousands of Southern Irishmen who hastened to the battle front . . . the approaches which the Southern Irish ports and airfields could so easily have guarded, were closed by the hostile aircraft and U–boats. This was indeed a deadly moment in our life, and if it had not been for the loyalty and friendship of Northern Ireland we should have been forced to come to close quarters or perish far from the earth. However, with a restraint and poise to which, I say, history will find few parallels, His Majesty's Government never laid a violent hand on them. . . . When I think of these days I also think of other episodes and personalities. I think of Lieutenant–Commander Esmonde, V.C., of Lance Corporal Keneally, V.C., and Captain Fegen, V.C., and other Irish heroes whose names I could easily recite, and then I must confess that bitterness by Britain against the Irish race dies in my heart.

Irrespective of Churchill's death of 'bitterness against the Irish race', one immediate post–war effect upon the Irish in Britain was to give them a sense of involvement in the general spectrum of British life. The comradeship which many developed in the fight for King and Country was reflected in business and personal relationships after the war. Many an Irish soldier found subsequent employment through the good offices of a war–time officer; some went into business partner–ship with former comrades–in–arms, notably in the construc–tion field, which now enjoyed a post–war boom of rebuilding. Another effect was the comparative 'reduction' of class–barriers and the assumption to power of the Labour party, with whom the Irish felt some degree of affinity; the city of Birmingham which contained a substantial Irish community returned a 23 per cent swing to Labour in the 1945 General Election. There were many other changes which encouraged the Irish to feel part of post–war Britain. The effects of the Education Act of 1944, which ensured equality of treatment to all religious denominations were noticed in the increased building of Catholic schools, and the Irish benefited equally from the successive Acts of Parliament which brought about the Welfare State.[13] During the war, wages had gone up con–siderably; an immediate post–war effect was the heightened resumption of immigration from Ireland to employment in the building sites and factories. Even the footloose were better off on the dole in England than in Ireland: Britain offered double the unemployment money. The vast majority, of course, came to work and to claim a stake in the new Britain, and many were pleasantly surprised to find that the post–war sense of

common weal encouraged that attitude. Out of this involvement came the founding of the Irish Club in London's
Eaton Square, an area more commonly identified with the
aristocracy, by a group of Irishmen who met sometime in 1947
in a hostelry by the Bank of England and decided that a focal
monument of similar impact was required as a gesture to the
future presence of the Irish. The substantial premises in Eaton
Square, equal distance almost from Buckingham Palace and
Westminster Catholic Cathedral, were acquired with the aid of
a donation from the Guinness family in 1948—the year that
the State of Eire formally declared herself a Republic. The
initial membership of the Eaton Square club reflected the
post–war growth of a weighty middle–class element among the
immigrants with some attendant social pretensions.

One personality who refused to join was Bernard Shaw
ever impatient with the sentimentality of the exiles. In a
characteristic reply by postcard, Shaw declared:

> I can imagine nothing less desirable than an Irish Club
> Irish people in England should join English clubs, and
> avoid each other like the plague.
> If they flock together like geese they might as well have
> never left Ireland.
> They don't admire, nor even like one another. In English
> clubs they are always welcome. More fools the English
> perhaps; but the two are so foreign that they have much
> to learn from their association and co–operation.
>
> G. Bernard Shaw

The Irish Club in fact became less introspective than Shaw
might have imagined; reflecting the composite interests of
retired Brigadiers, nouveau riche owners of building firms
and businessmen intent on bridging historical suspicions.[14] It
was a concerted effort on behalf of middle–class immigrant
to upgrade the popular residual image of Irish immigrants, or
in the words of one long–time member, the Club was an effort
to 'show the English that we weren't all navvies and chamber
maids', a double–edged comment hardly likely to endear the
Club to the mass of working–class Irish. The Club did help
'bridge the gap' in the ensuing years between the immigrant

classes, and later effected a wider diplomatic function; although an Irish Embassy became established in nearby Belgravia (in a former town–house of the Guinness family) a year after the Club became operational, the Club in fact functioned as a mini–embassy in many respects and was to be a hidden, but not insignificant, influence in subsequent Anglo–Irish relations. Not the least of its contributions was in creating the tradition whereby British and Irish Ministers of State became guests of honour at the annual St Patrick's Day dinner, thereby providing useful facilities for relaxed meetings between both Governments. Nevertheless its existence, and pretensions, aroused strong feelings in the Irish community. A former Club Chairman, Noel O'Connell, provides this view of Shaw's post–card refusal to join:

The Founding Fathers of the Irish Club were incurable optimists. They created the Club in a euphoria of goodwill and good intentions, never doubting the sense and sensibility of their idea. Shaw's postcard must have been a rude shock, dismissed no doubt as another of his crusty rejoinders. After all, Shaw was always wrong, wasn't he? Or was he?

Of course Shaw was hardly a typical immigrant. Not for him Euston in the grey dawn, digs in West Hampstead, insecurity for a period. He had the benefit of starting at the top and working his way down. It was really not too difficult for him 'to join English Clubs' (and he derived considerable advantage therefrom). His life, however, pinpoints the un-changing dilemma of adjustment for newcomers to any society – to 'integrate' (meaningless term) and still to main-tain the distinctive and valuable attributes of a different culture.

The nub of Shaw's postcard is his quite right view that the English and the Irish have each 'much to learn from their association and co-operation'. Shaw obviously feared that the Club would be 'forever Ireland' and nothing more. In this he has been proved very wrong indeed. Certainly for a number of members the Club is an introspective haven saving them from the realities of life in England and maintaining what they sadly believe to be a reflection of life in Ireland ('times remembered'). But they are the few. The majority see the Club as a place where Shaw's idea could be realized by making the Club the point of contact between the two cultures of the two islands, and by doing that from a position of strength rather than from weakness of solo efforts. The most difficult trait of the Anglo-Saxon to accept (and to change!) is his quiet assumption of superiority, bolstered frequently by comparing the best of England with the worst of other places. The Irish Club has not been excessively chauvinistic but has endeavoured to compare like with like, to display differences for enjoyment rather than for evaluation. And in the process, members of Shaw's English Clubs have commented so frequently how much they prefer ours.

Whatever the motives for the founding of the Club, its creation in 1948 nevertheless signified the emergence of an immigrant middle–class. Eaton Square, it could be said, was a long way from the embarkation sheds in Liverpool of the Famine diaspora. The journey was precisely that of a hundred years.

1950s

It is evident that much had changed in that century in relation to the status of the Irish. Although substantially unskilled, no longer were they totally such: 22 per cent were engaged in skilled occupations, according to the 1951 census. Neither were they, in the dormancy of the Ulster issue, excessively nationalistic. These changes meant less concentration by new arrivals upon the traditional areas of settlement, meant a more diffused absorption into the general fabric of Britain. In the early fifties, an increasing minority arrived with marketable skills, or with the intent of acquiring some, and shunned the traditional ghetto areas as places of abode. One immigrant of the fifties, now an advertising executive, told me:

'Camden Town or Hammersmith were two areas of London that I determined *not* to live in when I came to London in 1954. I didn't want to be identified with "The Paddies" – I

knew all about them before leaving Ireland. Anyway, what
was the point of coming to London, unless one met and got
to know English people. Mind you, I spent my first few
weeks feeling pretty miserable in a room in Earls Court. But
I gradually got to know people—Earls Court was like a
village then—and began to have fun. I didn't find any
prejudice regarding a job, answering an advertisement in the
London *Evening Standard* landed me into the production
department of an advertising agency, where I operated a
Gestetner duplicating machine for which I was paid eight
pounds a week. That was fantastic money to me, then – at
least twice what I would have earned in Ireland, and then
only if I knew someone with a bit of "pull" to get me appren-
ticed to a solicitor or something like that.

'Anyway, here I was at twenty-two with my own flat and
spending money; I had about four pounds to spend on
myself . . . or on girls, as it turned out. I had a fantastic
time with the girls at work, you know what English girls
are like . . . compared to Irish girls. Although I felt a bit
guilty at first, you know being a Catholic, I thought "when
in Rome . . .", what's the point of being in England unless
one enjoys it. So in a few months I had gone through half
the girls in the place and got a bit bored and concentrated
on the job. And then I ran up against my first bit of
prejudice – this supervisor started making anti–Irish cracks,
about the ports in the war and drunken Paddies and that
sort of thing. But you know, he only started that when I
began to point out his mistakes to him in the print–room!
That's how cocky I was then. So I moved to another agency
as production manager, where there was an even more
interesting crop of girls, though now I was beginning to get
a bit selective, wanting something on top as well, you know.
Of course, I went to Ireland on holiday every year, but I
was always damn glad to come back here and the fellows I
grew up with who hadn't left seemed terribly dull, really
stuck in a mediocre rut. Then at the advertising agency they
made me a junior executive, so I started watching my "P's
and Q's" then; I used to wear a stiff white collar and I
brushed–up my table manners, learned about wines and all

that rubbish – and it paid off. They made me an account executive. So why should I have lived in Camden Town or some Irish place? Mind you, my one true friend is Irish, and even many of my other friends are either of Irish descent, or have an Irish temperament. I'm not sensitive about my nationality, although nowadays some people don't take me as Irish; I'm not sensitive about phrases like 'bloody Irish at it again' which is what one sometimes hears about the North from people I do business with. After all, it's my job not to be offended.'

My informant, now the possessor of an elegant London apartment and a boat on the South Coast, represents the small but increasing proportion who came in the fifties, and were intent on not just mere survival but on positively exploiting the novel territories of their social, cultural, and intellectual expansion in Britain. Cracks began to appear in the century–old mould of lumpen proletarian immigration at different levels. By contrast with the previous decades, immigrant girls began to move away from domestic service and to receive training as nurses, and to a lesser extent as teachers. Men who in previous decades were content to remain as navvies now sought opportunities to become sub–contractors. Barmen served with an eye to the day when they might become landlord of their own premises. Greater numbers of both sexes were to be found in white–collar employment, attending evening classes in search of marketable credentials, and residing in middle–class districts. Higher and more widespread education in Ireland gave rise to new initiative which grafted onto the old émigré tradition a more positive approach to life in the new country. A pointer to future possibilities was provided by the town of Southampton when, in 1955, it elected as Mayor one Mollie O'Higgins, a Dubliner who had come to work as a 'clippie' on the buses in the First World War. In London an Irish employment agency was founded specializing in hotel and catering staff; some of those who first came on its books were subsequently to open their own hotels and restaurants. There were even some who came strictly on business: McConnell's Advertising Agency of Dublin, whose Chairman had been one of the founders of the Eaton Square Irish Club, expanded to Britain with branches in London and other cities. Eamonn Andrews, a young boxing commentator on Radio Eireann, was invited to audition for the B.B.C. and stayed on to chair the top–rating show of the time, 'What's My Line'. Other, less dramatic, examples came to work in publishing and journalism, in banks and insurance offices. One family made notable impact: Dominic Behan in the fifties was working as a housepainter by day and writing scripts in the evening for the B.B.C. Third Programme, where the poet Louis MacNeice and other expatriate Irish literati were enjoying something of a golden mein, inheritors to that tradition of émigré literary entertainer set by Congreve, Sheridan, Farquhar, Shaw, Wilde, O'Casey, and now Brendan Behan. In a restored Music Hall in the East End of London, the Theatre Royal at Stratford East where many a Famine-furtive 'Oirish' entertainer had appeared before the footlights to declaim (in effect): 'Laugh at me, I'm harmless', Brendan Behan's play *The Hostage* was, in the critic Kenneth Tynan's observation, 'an example of Ireland's function every twenty years or so to provide a playwright who will kick English drama from the past into the present'. Brendan Behan's other public capacity, for clowning and alcoholic binges, (the pressure–tap blowing on the mortal wounds within) exemplified, of course, to many the classic image of the immigrant Irishman, and much of the Behan saga did irretrievably connect with the strands of emigration; the playwright who was now fêted by the literary aristocracy had, as we have seen, been a Borstal Boy for I.R.A. offences in Liverpool. While he and his brother, Dominic, fulfilled one tradition, a third brother, Brian Behan, fulfilled another immigrant inheritance, that of Feargus O'Connor's Republican Socialism, or as it was more popularly known then in the fifties as 'left–wing agitation', which reflected the further diffusion of immigrant impact at an elementary level. The strike on London's South Bank in 1958 may be regarded as evidence of that trend.

The post–war building boom in Britain had continued into the fifties, notably with the construction of massive office blocks and commercial buildings, such as the Shell Building

D*

and the South Bank concrete complex. At least half the work forces on these massive sites were Irish; emigration from Ireland, in spite of social advances, was still running at upward of 40,000 per year. The labouring men from the rural areas of Connacht found work mainly on the building sites of the London South Bank and lived in the nearby Elephant and Castle slum districts, where it was not uncommon to hear Connemara Gaelic spoken in the public houses. The work was rough and tough, particularly in the pile–boring and in the excavation of the huge basins to take thousands of tons of liquid cement which today form the concrete foundations of the impressive building achievement. In Behan's lyrical recollection:

Round the edge of the crater the draglines lifted their iron necks and sent their teeth darting down like a great buzzard's beak. Remorselessly they tore at the ground and deeper and deeper grew the cavity ... then into it climbed the carpenters and steelfixers; on platforms ninety feet below ground they shored–up the avenging clay with struts of timber and steel. Then from a swan–like crane, with its rider perched one hundred and fifty feet up, came an endless golden, thick creamy porridge that will set rock–hard to carry the monster building on its back.

Such classical endeavour, to Brian Behan's radical political instincts, merely highlighted the hazards involved in the creation of 'capitalistic monuments' and seemed incongruous with the work and living conditions of those who laboured in their construction. Behan records: 'Four men died before that silly roof was stuck on, like a clown's hat atop a bear's head ... the men know that even if the firm is blameless it is always their own kind who lie crushed and mangled beneath the planner's beams.' Many a novice complainer in an Irish work gang, as Brian Behan remembers, 'was shut up with a belt across the face by an Irish foreman intent only on bonus profit for himself'. The system of individual work–gang bonuses which encouraged such bullying was but one of the work conditions which Behan campaigned against. As a former member of a turf-cutting gang in literally, the bogs of Ireland (where he had earned thirty shillings a week before emigrating), Behan was particularly sensitive to the evils of 'pitting worker against worker'. He became active as a strike–leader and his colourful turn of militant invective found support from among a minority of the Irish workforce. Some of his strongest supporters were drawn from the ranks of the clannish Connemara men, from Scots–Irish adherents of Keir Hardie, and included some former I.R.A. men from Belfast all of whom were instrumental in mounting a lock–out strike on the South Bank site, 'with the biggest ring–a–rosy picket on a building site the industry has ever witnessed', which culminated in a pitched battle with the police. Brian Behan served a prison sentence for 'incitement to riot', and was subsequently black–listed from sites by unions and employers alike.

The significance of the South Bank strike in Irish terms was that it characterized the 'diffusion' of the fifties, i.e. the moving out from the straitjacketed immigrant mentality of regarding themselves as mere economic fodder with no function other than that of a passive work–force. The trade union militancy of Irish workers was in part the product of disillusion with the administration in Ireland which had failed to provide employment in Ireland—all through the fifties the surplus of unemployed rarely fell below 40,000 a year and the 'dole' offered the magnificent weekly sum of thirty-four shillings. Many of the young men who left in that decade carried with them a political bitterness against their own native establishment which was to find expression in their lives in Britain, most notably in trade union involvement. Even for the soft underbelly of migrant construction workers, conditions and wages had enormously improved, partly due to the large–scale site strikes, but the most notable change in the pattern of the fifties lay with the diffusion of a previous near–total labouring force into more varied and improved employment. Accompanying this improvement was a noticeable dilution of anti–British feeling, a potent confirmation of change which was noted with some alarm in a confidential report of the Anti–Partition League in 1957. (The League had been active in Britain in the earlier years of the decade, attempting to mobilize the 850,000 Irish to influence the Ulster question as an electoral issue and was in receipt of a secret subvention from the Irish Government.) But in a decade of ostensible political peace between both countries membership had dwindled; discussing the causes of lapse of support, the national organizer Tadhg Feehan noted: 'A potentially influential number of Irish comprising the professional class or those doing well in business, are primarily concerned with securing a good social standing in their particular milieu. They remain, of course, Irish in most senses of the term and are quite happy to be identified with Irish functions of a social character. But they are not prepared either to take active steps in relation to partition or to be, at least publicly, identified with direct efforts to end it through action in this country. A second category which comprises the vast bulk of the Irish–born population, consists of those who are engaged in subordinate employment. Their primary concern is to make a living and, if possible, put some money aside. Indeed one hears stories, from priests and others with considerable experience of our compatriots in this country, of a striking absence of national sentiment in great numbers of the Irish–born population and particularly in the more recent and younger immigrants.'

The 'striking absence of national sentiment' may have been no more than the reaction of the older generation immigrant to the more pragmatic attitudes of those who came in the late fifties, and who were more intent on investigating and exploiting the new opportunities in Britain. Tri–colour flag-waving and lip–service to the sacred cows of the Republic, after all, had not provided them with the means to earn a living there, and many of the younger immigrants were impatient with such rhetoric. Indeed, for some Ireland was a dull place, depleted of manpower and initiative and appearing to offer little future challenge, whereas Britain by contrast offered work and, for many, the excitement of new terrain. It was an attitude of new positivism, characterized by a diffusion into more ambitious areas of employment and living and which—coinciding with the settlement progress of the previous generation—was to produce in the sixties the more independent community of the Other Irish.

Part Three

THE IRISH NOW

The Irish Now

The decade of 1960–70, marking the end of a century of relentless Irish immigration to Britain, marked also the beginning of a decade more fruitful for the Irish than any other time in the previous century's diaspora. The 'new positivism' of many of the Irish during this period was due mainly to increased levels of education and living standards in Ireland and encouraged them—against a background of political peace between both countries—to involve themselves more productively in the life of their adopted country.

Many factors combined to encourage their enhanced status, not least the radical changes in Britain during the sixties which dovetailed with the improved changes in the Irish. The falling-away from imperial attitudes in Britain was reflected in politics, in the media, and in the country at large, with an accelerated closing of the gap in earning–power between the working– and middle–classes. In politics, the speech of Conservative Prime Minister Harold Macmillan on 'The Winds of Change' (delivered in South Africa with the tired, if prudent, air of one who fears the spectacle of restless servants brandishing kitchen knives in the drawing–room) affirmed the growing inevitability of colonial disintegration. In the media, a similar internal disintegration was voiced in the emergence of the so-called 'kitchen–sink' writers such as John Osborne, Alan Sillitoe, Shelagh Delany *et al.*, now trenchantly demanding that the plaintiff voice of the kitchen be heard in the drawing–room.

These writers allied themselves with the burgeoning 'meritocracy' which revived the Labour party in the early sixties, articulating as they did the strident voice of those who took pride in being working–class (or variations thereof)

94

and who now asked to occupy the recesses of power formerly the sanctum of the traditionally better-off.

And the Irish, by now an equally burgeoning 'meritocracy' (though formerly the most hidebound of the habitués of Britain's kitchens) found that the egalitarian changes provided ideal cover from which to move tentatively out and upwards into the opportunistic sixties. As an immigrant people in the Britain of the sixties they were less subject to hostility, and more the object of tolerance—if not affection—than at any time in the long history of their diaspora to Britain. How they reacted to that radically-changed circumstance is the scope of the remainder of this book.

6

In Politics

A rough beast slouches toward Bethlehem to be born
—William Butler Yeats

One of the most immediate effects of the upgrading of the Irish community in the sixties was to be perceived in the political arena. Their new social solidity encouraged the emergence of a political involvement in domestic British politics: by the sixties almost every major local authority had Irish–born representation. This was most strong in the traditional immigrant areas, but in the less obvious districts the Irish who were members of the Labour party were encouraged to stand for election, an important factor being the personal encouragement provided by first and second generation Irish, now more secure in their own integrated identity and happily free of the pressure of the 'Irish Question' which had deflected loyalties previously.*

Accordingly, when Irish candidates went forward at local elections in the sixties, their interests were not to do with the 'Irish Question' (then dormant) but rather with local issues of housing, education, amenities, and such. Many indeed played down their Irishness and campaigned on matters of broad party policy. For most Irish candidates there was no conscious 'Irish Vote' to woo, except for those wishing to represent areas of traditional immigration, and here the Irish vote was coupled more to issues of specific interest such as schools, with an absence of overt Catholic pressure. There was little electoral

---

* Of the 363 Labour Members of Parliament who formed the majority in the House of Commons from 1966-70, around 35 were of immigrant Irish descent.

guidance from church pulpits; one priest in a Middlesbrough ward saw the distinction as: 'Taking our religion from Rome, but our politics from our bellies'. This gut reaction was more Irish than Catholic, in the sense that the mass of the Irish immigrants were, in British terms, working–class voters. Their natural antipathy to 'the gentry' of the Conservative party was compounded by the links which that party maintained with the Unionist Government of Northern Ireland. Though the middle–classes of the Irish in Britain tended to vote Con–servative, the majority of the immigrants who exercised the vote were loyal to the Labour party even when they moved marginally up the socio–economic scale.

This traditional loyalty was given a tremendous boost by the return to power of Labour administration in 1964 and by the subsequent activities of a Cabinet in which the names of Healey, Brown, and Callaghan invoked secure echoes in Irish pubs and clubs all over Britain. And not only did that 'holy trinity' make much and effective use of their Irish ancestry in public speeches, but the administration which they strongly influenced helped bring about a rapport between the Governments of Ireland and England unequalled in recent history. The high–lights of this rapport were: (a) the payment by the British authorities of pensions and other social security benefits to workers returned to Ireland (who were formerly domiciled in Britain). (b) The signing of the Anglo–Irish Free Trade Agreement, which provided for wider trade between both countries. (c) The return to Irish soil of 'patriot' remains, notably those of Sir Roger Casement: mystic, adventurer, and ex–colonial civil servant. Casement had been hanged as a traitor fifty years earlier, on a charge of running guns to Ireland to aid the rebels of the Republic declared in 1916. It is a telling commentary on the contrasting historical perspec–tives of the Irish *vis–à–vis* the English that the name Casement would draw a blank from most British, while invoking among Irish revered memories of a martyred patriot.) The remains of Barnes and McCormick, executed in connection with the I.R.A. bomb explosion in Coventry, were also returned during the Labour administration.

If politics is about people–management, then the Labour

Government of the mid–to–late sixties were masters of that art in relation to the Irish in Britain. The artifice which could initiate four pop singers into the Order of the British Empire (largely defunct) extended to the million or so politically sullen Irish in Britain. Successive St Patrick's Day dinners at plush hotels were graced by British Cabinet Ministers proposing the toast of 'The Two Islands' and in towns and cities all over Britain, local Labour dignitaries made known their willingness to attend Irish functions. It was a high time for the emerging Irish, coming out 'from under the shadow of the still rock' and into the warm glaze of acceptance. It was a time that coincided with increased economic affluence and productivity in Ireland, and a time of similar upgrading of the Irish in Britain, who were, for instance, moving from the tenements of dilapidated areas into council housing and the suburbs. It was also a time when the economic boom in Ireland had effect upon the quality of immigrants, and consequently upon the attitude of the host community. One immediate effect of the new industrialization in Ireland was that the more criminally–prone adolescents stayed at home to work in the new factories rather than head for Coventry or Birmingham. (The police in Ireland now found themselves facing an increase in the sort of urban crime more familiar to their British counterparts.)

The media exposure of such bodies as the Irish Tourist Board and Aer Lingus also helped upgrade the image of the Irish in Britain, although their colour–supplement purveyance of deserted rural beauty produced predictable wry reaction among those driven from such uneconomic pastures, ('You can't eat the scenery'). Most pertinently of all, the sharpening focus upon the increasing coloured immigrants distracted attention away from the Irish as an alien presence. With cyclic inevitability, coloured immigrants became the object of the same hostile platitudes of 'separateness', i.e. large families, eating habits, noisy parties, that the Irish had been subject to in previous generations. It was noticeable during the early sixties the extent to which the accommodation notices in shop windows translated the slogan 'No Irish' to that of 'No Coloureds' and how that barometer of popular agitation, Speakers' Corner in London, lost its rabble of tri–colour flags

and slogans to the invective of Black Power. Whereas in previous decades the issue of Northern Ireland had been a lively
one at Speakers' Corner, by the mid–sixties only a handful of
weary Republicans clustered around the ideal of a United
Ireland.

Towards the end of the previous century the Irish vote had
been profoundly affected by events in Ireland; so now in the
sixties was it equally affected by a radically changed situation
in Ireland.

The situation in the sixties which affected the immigrants
was that the Republic was bent on economic expansion,
luring in foreign industrialists with lucrative financial grants.
And with some success, to the extent of slicing the British–
bound emigration rate in the latter half of the sixties from
around 50,000 to 25,000 annually. Britain being the principal
outlet for exports, and with the new entente cordiale with the
Labour administration rampant, the last thing the young go–
getters of Fianna Fail wished to raise was the old spectre of
'Ulster under British Domination'. And the governing party
—Fianna Fail—now led by the pragmatic Sean Lemass,
perceived the patriotism of the slide–rule and financial balance
sheet to be more relevant to the needs of the majority of the
citizens in its care. So much so that when an Irish Cabinet
Minister of the period was questioned by a journalist on the
plight of Catholics in the North of Ireland, the bland reply
was: 'Ah, we don't worry about them. Sure the English
Catholic M.P.s at Westminster will look after them.'

The Irish Minister for Education on a St Patrick's Day
visit to an Irish university graduates' club in London in 1966
urged his audience to involve themselves in the constitutional
life in Britain. He told them: 'You must participate fully in
the affairs of the country of your adoption. You cannot be full
citizens of both countries.' His timing was impeccable, for his
exhortation came at a time when the Irish in Britain had
become assured and settled. They were moving out from the
ghetto mentality, making inroads into the mainstream of
national life, buying pubs and founding construction firms,
leaving the decaying city centres for the suburbs. They were
the largest single ethnic group in Britain and slowly and

reluctantly they were beginning to realize that for most of them there would be no 'going home next year'; that they were here to stay.

One obvious corollary was political involvement, initially at local council level, and in 1969 came the culmination of this 'infiltration', with the election of Mr Michael O'Halloran as Member of Parliament for the London constituency of Islington North. His election is of importance, for he is a man very much of his own émigré people. He owed his candidature not only to his long-standing service on Islington Council, but in some measure also to the influence of the Irish in the local Labour party selection committee, and to that lobby's determination that 'it was about time we had one of our own in the House'. In demeanour and personality O'Halloran is representative of the broad mass of Irish immigrants to Britain, having modest formal education, and having retained, after twenty years, his unmistakable accent. His election is significant, for it marks the breakthrough of the Irish immigrant into the constitutional life of the nation and the acceptance of that community by the establishment.

Most pertinent of all, O'Halloran's election to Westminster—for centuries a bane in the minds of the Irish—provided impetus for almost a million Irish-born to vote for candidates in the 1970 General Election. According to a survey published in the *Irish Post* after the election, 84 per cent of the 'Irish vote' had been cast in favour of Labour party candidates. It is worth relating that assertion to the contemporary awareness of the Ethnic vote.

THE IRISH 'ETHNIC VOTE' has been largely underestimated by British political parties. The Labour party had been marginally more conscious of the possibilities of the Irish vote for a variety of reasons; not least of these being the prominence of Irish-born and 'Brit-Irish' personalities in a number of powerful trade unions. In the run-up to the Election of 1970, both parties became aware of the Irish vote through the storm-clouds of the Ulster issue and its effects upon Irish voters in Britain.

In the run–up to that election, the twenty–five constituencies with potentially decisive Irish voting power were:

CONSTITUENCY		IRISH PERCENTAGE OF POPULATION
Willesden East	– London	14.5%
Hammersmith	– London	10.9%
Ardwick	– Manchester	10.1%
Willesden West	– London	10.0%
Kensington North	– London	9.6%
Islington North	– London	9.5%
Paddington North	– London	9.3%
Gorbals	– Glasgow	9.2%
Barons Court	– London	9.0%
Sparkbrook	– Birmingham	8.7%
St Pancras North	– London	8.6%
Paddington South	– London	8.5%
Moss Side	– Manchester	8.1%
Ladywood	– Birmingham	7.9%
Small Heath	– Birmingham	7.6%
Coventry South	– Coventry	7.6%
Acton	– London	7.3%
Hampstead	– London	7.3%
Selly Oak	– Birmingham	7.1%
Handsworth	– Birmingham	6.9%
Holborn/ St Pancras	– London	6.8%
All Saints	– Birmingham	6.7%
Exchange	– Manchester	6.6%
Islington East	– London	6.5%
Coventry North	– Coventry	6.5%

In the General Election, 18 June 1970, a Conservative Government was returned on a national voting swing of *4.7 per cent.* Even allowing for a margin of 'variables' due to re–housing and other demographic changes since 1966, it is clear that most of the above constituencies could have been heavily influenced by the Irish vote. In the event, and in the

face of a national voting swing toward Conservative candidates
of 4.7 per cent, *twenty of the above twenty-five* constituencies
returned a *Labour* candidate. (In at least two of the constituencies which returned a *Conservative* candidate, the
members had strong personal rapport with the Irish in the
constituency.)

It would be rash to conclude that, of those twenty-five
named constituencies with the highest Irish percentage of
voters, the twenty who returned Labour candidates did so
critically on the Irish vote. But in the light of other circum-
stantial evidence, it is clear that the Irish ethnic vote can no
longer be disregarded. In two Birmingham constituencies, for
example, the Conservative members hold their seats on a
swing of less than 2 per cent, yet the Irish–born form 7 per
cent of each constituency's electorate. In their definitive work
on the 1970 General Election[17], the authors David Butler and
Michael Pinto–Duschinsky decided that three seats in the
South–East were definitely decided by the Irish vote, while
the political colouring of another five seats possibly resided
with the Irish. Even with the recent re–drawing of constituency
boundaries, around thirty parliamentary seats could be decided
by the *en bloc* Irish vote. Given that Irish–born form around
2 per cent of the population, and that those thirty seats represent around 5 per cent of the total allocation, it would appear
that the immigrants form a potential electoral power disproportionate to their numbers. This is one of the unforeseen
advantages of the ghetto–grouping, proving a belated pay–off
for the miseries of the nineteenth–century slum settlements,
and the tradition bred therefrom.

What is notably different from the political attitudes of those
settlements is the relative absence of clerical influence in rela–
tion to current Irish voting attitudes on domestic British issues.
Except in the case of the Ulster issue, Irish priests display but
minimum interest and influence in relation to the party political
attitudes of their compatriots. Even such a potentially emotive
issue as the Abortion Act of 1967, by which a Labour administration legalized surgical pregnancy terminations, did not
arouse any meaningful Irish Catholic lobby in electoral terms.
It is true that various Catholic lobbies opposed the measure,

lobbies such as the Union of Catholic Mothers, but these were representative of general Catholic attitudes rather than of specific immigrant interest. The Birmingham constituency of Perry Barr provides a case in point.

Prior to the General Election of 1970, the Labour party incumbent was Christopher Price, who had supported the movement for Abortion Law Reform. In the year prior to the Election, his Conservative opponent Joseph Kinsey had formulated a rapport with influential sections of the Birmingham-Irish community and had been instrumental in securing the lease of a local hall for use as Irish club premises. Remembering that the Irish generally voted Labour, the Conservative Kinsey was returned on a swing of 12.6 per cent; and local observers judge him to have netted most of the available Irish vote, not so much as a reaction to the Labour candidate's identity with the Abortion Bill, but more because of his sympathetic assistance to the Irish community on practical welfare matters. There are other such examples which suggest that the Irish vote is not heavily vulnerable to issues of abstract Catholic morality, but is subject rather to a straight functional influence of a candidate's rapport with the Irish community, and what that community feels it may tangibly receive in return for its vote! The Irish in Britain are historically conditioned towards a pragmatic use of their vote, a reaction originating in the parish–pump 'you scratch my back: I'll scratch yours' level of politics in Ireland.

They are not susceptible, generally speaking, to appeals of broad or abstract philosophical difference. They have traditionally voted Labour because that party traditionally reflected what the Irish deemed to be most close to their own material interests in Britain. It was under cautious Labour party encouragement that they have emerged as a present–day influential—and potentially weighty—factor in the political life of their adopted country. Not the least significant implication of that 'slouching towards Bethlehem to be born' political emergence is the pointer towards future political participation of other ethnic minorities. At the local elections of May 1971, for instance, over 150 Irish candidates presented themselves to the electorate; a hundred more than the previous time.

Three–quarters of them stood for Labour. In Michael O'Halloran's constituency of Islington North, six Irish–born candidates were elected. In Luton another six of the forty-eight member council were Irish–born. At the time of writing the Irish occupy the office of Mayor in three British boroughs —Luton, Derby, and Kettering. A look at one of these personalities, the Mayor of Luton, is relevant, for like O'Halloran, he epitomizes the upward movement of the Irish.

James Cussen, fifty-year-old Mayor of Luton, emigrant from Limerick is now a comfortable partner in a Luton building firm. It wasn't always like that. For James Cussen, emigrant, came to England in 1939, a time of severe economic depression in Ireland. He was just one of a batch of migrant workers who crossed the Irish Sea and—this being wartime —were directed to whatever strategic area in which labour was required. He was sent to Northampton, to help build an airfield. As he remembers it: 'We were billeted in a nissen hut, all Irish lads just over. When the air–raid warning went we thought we were being bombed. We had no training in this sort of thing, so we made like the clappers for the door and ran out all over the fields. And some must have kept running, for there were a few missing the following morning.'

From that first introduction to Britain, coming down in the blacked–out train from the entry port of Holyhead and working on the aerodrome, Cussen went to Luton to look for 'digs' in one of the many 'Irish Houses' in the area. He found work in a local factory, walked out with the landlady's daughter and joined the local Young Socialists, 'more for the social company than the ideas. I was a raw immigrant and when someone at work said come along for a drink and a chat, I was glad to. Of course, having left Ireland at the end of the thirties when things were really bad, I had never heard of such phrases as "social justice". Mind you, I knew what social injustice meant, even if I couldn't always describe it. I knew what it meant to go to school in shoe–leather when most of my classmates were barefoot.' His attendance at the Young Socialists gave him political ambitions, but when he went to stand as a Labour candidate after the war he ran up against an unexpected obstacle. The factory where he worked made it plain that his job rating would suffer if he were elected. Cussen remembers: 'They didn't like the idea of a worker having influence on the council, so I withdrew my application to stand.' It is an indicative irony that, twenty–five years later, management representatives of the same Luton firm were happy to attend the mayoral inauguration. Cussen married the landlady's daughter, one Eve O'Connor, and at the mayoral reception he replaced the usual string quartet with a ceili band.

The town he represents, Luton, has a population of 150,000 centred on the car industry, with an Irish colony of 15,000. In some areas of the town, whole streets are not only Irish, but are occupied by immigrants from particular towns in Ireland, so that an intensely clannish air pervades these areas. To the extent that, as one resident put it, 'If someone comes over from the west of Ireland looking for a job, he only has to mention what town he comes from and I'll know what street to direct him to.'

The Irish are so ingrained in the fabric of Luton (it being one of the stops outside London on the Great North Road during the mass migration of the post–famine travellers) that there was scant opposition to the prospect of an Irish mayor. Which is in some contrast to the election of Paddy O'Connor as Mayor of Camden some years previously (at a time when the borough had become enlarged to include the upper middle-class areas of Hampstead). The correspondence columns of the local paper were the platform of a raging controversy as to the propriety of an English borough, albeit Camden, having an Irish mayor. Perhaps the closing comment should be that the then Mayor of Camden, Paddy O'Connor, is the brother of the 'landlady's daughter', Eve O'Connor, who married the present Mayor of Luton! Again, the significance of Cussen is that he is a traditional emigrant, having come to labour and stayed on to be mayor. And though he holidays in Ireland every year, his roots are more with the Irish in Britain; with his family, his church and his community. He is part of that separate 'Middle Nation' of the Irish, and perhaps as such embraces more of the virtues of the Irish–English than their respective vices and has obviously been enriched by the process of emigration.

What, it may be asked, has been the response of the other principal British political party to the dominant support among the Irish for the Labour party? Until the General Election of 1970, the Conservatives were content to allow the Labour party to make all the running with the Irish. Not that the Conservative party was without Irish connections, particularly in the persons of Sir Toby O'Brien (an influential figure in Tory Central Office), Norman St John Stevas M.P., and further back, former premier Harold Macmillan. But those connections were regarded, somewhat unfairly, as being with the Ascendancy (Anglo–Irish) and certainly the mass of the Irish in Britain regarded them as being far removed from themselves. The vast majority of the immigrants were and are from the southern Republic of Ireland; their natural antipathy towards Tories is compounded by the links which that party maintains with the Unionist Government of Northern Ireland, links enshrined in the official title of 'The Conservative and Unionist Party'. The extent of Irish support for Labour became a source of some concern to the hierarchy at Conservative Central Office in their intelligence operation prior to the last General Election. (During the sixties an emerging minority of Irish businessmen and new middle class gravitated towards the Tories, mainly motivated by resentment at what was considered to be penal taxation by the Socialists. Shortly before the General Election, with the Conservative promise to return an Immigration Bill if brought to power, a particular Irish-dominated Conservative party in the provinces made known to Central Office that if the Irish were included in the Bill there would be no cars to get the vote out on polling day!) Once the election was won, consideration of the 'Irish vote' came to fruition with the establishment of the Irish Conservative Association which has as its long-term objective, 'the improvement of communication between the Irish in Britain and the Conservative party'. The Association has the blessing of Central Office—the powerhouse of the Tory party—and its founder is Paul Dwyer. Dwyer, a Hammersmith councillor, has all the moneyed elegance of the British upper class, allied to an acute awareness of his own Irish ancestry. It was this dichotomy, so to speak, between his socio–political position and his awareness of the traditional Labour party hold over the immigrant Irish vote that led to his founding the Irish Conservative Association. No one in political circles doubts that the salient long–term objective of the Association is to wean the immigrant Irish Vote away from Labour.

In its short life-span of two years, the Association has formulated the basis of what may well emerge as a significant power–structure of the Irish in Britain, simply because the formal organization exists whereby the various grass–roots interests of the Irish may be communicated to the Conservative Government of the day. It is something totally new for the rank–and–file Irish to be thus represented. Within months of its founding, the Irish Conservative Association was instrumental in handing over to a housing trust, SHAC,[18] the tenure of short–life properties in London. In the London borough of Hammersmith, it set up a community advice centre to act as go–between for the council and those in need of welfare advice.

It sees help with housing as a major contribution, a relevant priority in view of the propensity of the Irish to have, compared with other immigrant groups, the largest number of children per family. Comparisons may be odious, but if politics are often about the record of one party *vis–à–vis* another, the Association has yet to make the dramatic impact akin to the Labour party rapport of the early sixties. Though I have it on good authority that there was an offer, via the Irish Conservative Association, that the Conservative Prime Minister, Edward Heath, would be happy to attend the annual Gaelic Games in Wembley Stadium, it is a measure of the still entrenched insularity of grass–roots Irish towards the Conservatives that *such an invitation was not forthcoming from the Irish,* and is unlikely to be until the utopia of a United Ireland is declared!

In the meantime, the Irish Conservative Association is unlikely to suffer from the absence of such dramatic declarations. The mass of the Irish in Britain are more concerned with the minutiae of day–to–day living in the country of their adoption, and it is in such areas of help with housing and welfare that the Irish Conservative Association could woo some of the immigrant Irish. That, and an increasing involvement of the Irish in Britain in the general life of the Conservative party would appear to be the pointer for the future, for the rooted Irish in Britain, increasingly weathered in the mores of the British way of life, see parliamentary participation as the only valid way forward. As one staunch supporter of the Association said to me (himself a former Republican activist in Ireland, but now a prosperous leader of the community in Britain): 'We are here to stay. It only makes sense that we should do business with the party that for at least half of our lifetime will form the Government of Britain.'

His thinking is echoed by the growing support of a section of the Irish, mainly businessmen, for the Tories. The initiator of the movement, Paul Dwyer, has already extended this support beyond the business community, at least in terms of his own personal support. In the London local elections of May 1971, when the electorate moved massively to Labour, Dwyer held on to his Tory seat on Hammersmith Council and reckons to have been helped in this by gaining 99 per cent of the Irish vote in his ward. (It is pertinent to record, of course, that the Tory motivation in wooing the Irish is to a large extent due to the upgrading of this ethnic voting power by the Labour party since the 1920s. This Labour encouragement was less calculated than the present Tory motivation. But such is the nature of politics.) The growth of the Conservative–Irish Association, perhaps more than the election of Michael O'Halloran, signified the changed relationship of the émigrés in the sixties, marking a degree of political independence free from inherited attitudes and being specifically an offspring of a tentative affair between the Establishment and the immigrants. The Association thus became the first political casualty of the revolution in Ulster; following the Derry shootings of January 1972, the *Irish Post*, which has previously supported and publicized the efforts of the Irish–Conservative Association, called for the resignation of 'those Irish people who are members of the Conservative party'. With an about–face the paper added: 'Toryism and the Irish in Britain never had much in common – it is now repugnant that they should even breathe the same air.'

ULSTER AND THE IRISH IN BRITAIN

In contemplating political attitudes since the early nineteenth century, it is clear that the immigrants were swayed more by events in Ireland than in Britain. A necessary by-product of the political calm of the early sixties was the near extinction of the various organizations which had formerly campaigned for a United Ireland in the forties and fifties. Chief casualty was the Anti–Partition (Border) League which had flourished in the forties. By the late fifties its National Organizer had gone off to a comfortable sinecure in the Irish Embassy in London. The Connolly Association, under the devoted and indefatigable Desmond Greaves, continued to lobby M.P.s at Westminster, hold 'teach–ins', and fitfully published its organ of Connolly philosophy, *The Irish Democrat*. Former I.R.A. men (including some veterans of the 1939 Bombing Campaign) reminisced in pubs and gathered for meagre ritual nostalgia at Speakers' Corner in Hyde Park. Some 'bridged the gap' by joining the Labour party. The political running of the Irish was now in the constitutional hustings of local politics. Then, in October 1968, the slumbering mad–dog of the Republican conscience awoke, prodded to life by the batons of the Royal Ulster Constabulary—and by the fortuitous presence of one television cameraman—during a Civil Rights march in Londonderry. The effects of the subsequent escalation upon the Irish here may be summarized:

1968: The Derry disturbances catalysed the dormant political consciousness. The Connolly Association stepped–up lobbying of M.P.s, followed by other organizations such as the Campaign for Democracy in Ulster, the United Ireland Association, and other minority groupings.

1969: The establishment of a British section of the Northern Ireland Civil Rights Association which attempted to unify the disparate organizations under a 'Civil Rights' umbrella with some success. But the attacks upon Belfast Catholic enclaves stimulated more individualistic reaction. Eamon Smullen, a trade union official and Republican Socialist was sentenced to a term of imprisonment following an alleged attempt to purchase arms in Huddersfield. Collections were made on building sites and funds remitted to Catholic areas of Derry and Belfast. The split in the Republican Movement in Ireland was reflected in a similar division among Republicans in Britain into the camps of the Provisional and Official I.R.A. As the sparsely-attended Hyde Park gatherings of the sixties swelled visibly

against the flaring emotions of Northern Ireland, the ragged
straggle of marchers to Trafalgar Square took on a new vigour.
(One of the more bizarre aspects of Republican marches in
Britain is to hear a visiting Republican leader from Dublin
vehemently denounce Westminster under the impassive protection of the London Metropolitan Police. And then, without
geographic accuracy, I have seen the President of Sinn Fein,
standing in Trafalgar Square with his back to Westminster,
point an accusing political finger at, in effect, the National
Gallery!) Some incensed and footloose young men returned to
man the barricades in the Catholic enclaves. Both the Ulster
Office and the Irish Embassy became the target of demonstrations, but the great mass of the Irish immigrants remained
outwardly quiescent.

1970: Increased Ulster warfare produced attendant militancy
in Britain. In July a C.S. gas canister was tossed into the
debating chamber of the House of Commons and a twenty-
seven-year-old native of Wexford, James Anthony Roche, was
subsequently sentenced to eighteen months' imprisonment. In
the following month of August, Special Branch Officers raided
a house in Tooting, South London, and uncovered what was
later alleged to be an I.R.A. bomb—making cell. Grim echoes
of the Bombing Campaign of 1939 were evoked by headlines
in the mass—circulation newspapers, a recall made more potent
by an explosion a short time later of a bomb being taken from
a London cinema. At the trial of the Tooting men, however,
it was stated by the leader of the group, Brendan Magill, that
no repetition of the war bombing had been envisaged by the
I.R.A. group of which he was a self—confessed officer. Police
evidence, on the other hand, asserted that the materials found
were for use against the C.S. gas factory at Dorking, Surrey.

In contrast to previous convictions of I.R.A. men in Britain,
Magill was fortunate in receiving a comparatively light sentence
of two years. Magill, thirty-seven at the time of his conviction
and a family man with an English wife and five children, was
the owner of a prosperous antique furniture business. He had
lived a law—abiding life in Britain for fifteen years until the
trauma of his native Northern Ireland awoke a Republicanism
that was to land him in the dock.

The man who startled the Commons with a spluttering of C.S. gas, James Roche, was similarly moved to action by events in Ulster. A member of the Marxist–orientated Irish Solidarity Campaign which is entirely a British–based organization, Roche had made two unsuccessful attempts to complete a university graduation but had been frustrated by a combination of personal impatience and lack of funds. He had worked in factories in London where his political sense had involved him in trade–union agitation and in the months preceding the House of Commons incident he had been on the barricades in Derry with Bernadette Devlin. Apart from the incident in Parliament, he is pinned into historical fabric by his very name, Roche; the Irish provincial town in which he was born has long been dominated by the Roche Castle of the Norman Conquest of Henry II, the conquest which marked the original British presence in Ireland.

For those who like to perceive such historical undercurrents, the organization of which he is an active leader, the Irish Solidarity Campaign, consists of an almost even split between English student socialists, left–wingers, and Irish students in Britain. Roche's parliamentary debut, in fact, served as an effective blast upon the organization's recruiting trumpet, with the *Guardian* newspaper account of the incident subsequently becoming a party–piece in British left–wing university circles. It is heard to best effect when delivered with a *sotto voce* emphasis upon the italicized phrases (my italics, not the *Guardian*'s).

'Any panic which the 100 M.P.s present might have felt was swamped by their total disbelief. During the 30 seconds between the throwing of the canister and the rising of the smoke only Mr Andrew Faulds, Labour M.P. for Smethwick and traditionally the noisiest member of the House, got up. Mr Tom Swain, Labour M.P. for Derbyshire North–East, who was sitting near him on the front bench below the gangway, tried to stamp out the smouldering canister, but he was overcome by smoke. Mr Swain, aged 58, who has already suffered a serious heart attack this year, was later taken to Westminster Hospital.

'(The Speaker, Dr Horace King, was seen from farther along

the gallery to have collapsed in his chair. Sir Robert Grant–Ferris, Deputy Speaker, said later: "I grabbed him by both arms, pulled him from the chair, and assisted him out of the back of the Chamber".)

'Soon the smoke had risen to the level of the front benches – and the smell of the Bogside and stinging, unreal tears came to all our eyes.

'Mr Anthony Barber cut short his statement on the Common Market and *left the Chamber quickly.*

'Mr Robert Carr who had just made a statement on the future of the Prices and Incomes Board, crouched beneath the dispatch box *with his parliamentary secretary, Mr Dudley Smith.*

'Mrs Barbara Castle who a few minutes earlier had accused Mr Carr of personal and political vindictiveness, fled from the Chamber *without her handbag.*

'She was followed by her front-bench colleagues: Mr. George Thomson who was about to answer the Common Market statement; Mr Fred Peart, former Leader of the House; and Mr Mellish, Opposition Chief Whip, who had been only a few inches from the second canister. Later Mr Mellish said: "It was right under my feet, the first one. I thought it was a hand grenade. I ran. I went like a bomb. *I wasn't going to read my bloody obituary in The Times".*

'. . . The Speaker's bewigged clerks brought up the rear muttering: "*Sitting suspended*."

'Mr John Biggs–Davidson (C. Chigwell) said afterwards that he and the Serjeant–at–Arms had gone towards the canister to stamp it out. "I tried to approach it but got lost in gas. My face was burning, my eyes running, and I was retching – and out I went."

'The Chamber was uninhabitable for two hours and when M.P.s came back coughing at 6.30 p.m. they were forced to hold handkerchiefs over their faces.

'Meanwhile, in the police room which overlooks New Palace Yard, the man was being questioned by the Attorney–General, Sir Peter Rawlinson. Eventually, without his shirt but wearing a jacket, he was bundled into a police van bound for Cannon Row. He was accompanied by a wastepaper basket containing the two burnt out canisters.

'Back in the Commons, the Speaker announced: "I have to inform the House that the man who caused the disturbance was taken into custody by the Serjeant–at–Arms, and I have directed that he be given into custody of the civil police."

'Mr Barber got up and started his statement again. But this time the public gallery was closed. The burn on the carpet a few inches from where he stood and the smarting eyes of his colleagues were the only evidence that *something strange had happened*.'*

* * *

By the end of 1970, the worsening Ulster situation had produced in Britain no less than a dozen political organizations, representing an equal disparity of political attitude. The partly-successful effort of the previous year by the London Executive of the Northern Ireland Civil Rights Association to unite these elements now collapsed under the weight of individual passions. It may be worth recording the organizations which attempt to 'politicize' the Irish in Britain in relation to Ulster.

The Connolly Association, in existence since the 1930s. Though its purveying of Connolly Socialism had earned it the alarmist odium of parish priests in Ireland—'a front for Communism'—the Association alone upheld a doctrine of concerned political involvement with the immigrants. Probably the most influential of all the organizations, in the context of long–term political influence.

United Ireland Association is a descendant of the Anti–Partition League of the 1940s; mainly composed of middle-aged, middle–class members it has provided a comfortable outlet over the generations for immigrant emotional indulgence in the idea of a United Ireland.

Irish Republican Army, interestingly enough, is not an illegal organization in Britain. The British wing followed the ideological division of 1969 into 'Provisionals' and 'Officials'. The latter section in Britain tends to attract the more politically educated and thoughtful, with a broadly–based political attitude towards Ulster. By contrast the Provisionals purvey a more

---

* From a report by Christine Eade in the *Guardian* of 24 July 1970.

E

simplistic solution of military strategy, but the hard core of both groups in Britain consist of trained veterans of previous guerilla campaigns in Ireland. Brendan Magill, arrested in Tooting, South London, in 1970 was, at the time of his conviction, chief of the British–based Provisional I.R.A. Both organizations hardly command two hundred members nationwide—a minute proportion of the one million Irish–born in Britain.

Irish Solidarity Campaign is a Marxist–oriented grouping of Irish and British members. At the time of writing, joint leaders are Bernadette Devlin and James Roche of C.S. gas note. A march in Glasgow organized in September 1971 by I.S.C. resulted in sectarian violence, during which a police inspector was slashed with that traditional Glasgow weapon, the open razor. Again, the organization hardly numbers more than 200 active members, nationwide.

Irish National Liberation Solidarity Front is the creation of one Edward Davoren, a young veteran of student protest at the London School of Economics. Following a Maoist line of analysis, and harking on the slogan: 'Political power comes out of the barrel of a gun', the organization is noted for the violence of its slogans and speeches, not least in its liberal use of the transatlantic impact of the term 'pig' to denote policemen. Apart from the Ulster issue it has attempted to capitalize on what it terms 'police harassment of working–class people' – without success. Total national support hardly exceeds 200.

Campaign for Social Justice in Northern Ireland, by contrast with the preceding London–based movements, is mainly active in Birmingham where, during 1970, it held meetings and marches at the rate of one a month. Maintaining a wide cross-section of support from among immigrants in Birmingham, its activities were somewhat limited following the imprisonment of its organizer, Tom McDowell, in Ulster during 1971.

Campaign for Democracy in Ulster works entirely with the parliamentary lobby and reflects the traditional alignment of British left–wing Labour thinking with Irish self–determination. Activists include Paul Rose, Labour M.P. for a Manchester constituency. Its political platform is one of 'Democracy in Ulster', rather than abolition of the Border.

These were the organizations, which during 1970, in Britain the 'umbrella' Northern Ireland Civil Rights Association attempted to blend into a cohesive force. In the Irish tradition of acrimony, it failed. In terms of impact upon the Irish community generally, the significant observation is that the total number of active followers of the above combined organizations do not exceed twenty-five thousand, or 2½ per cent of the total immigrant Irish community.

1971: Any survey of that year of bitter sectarian bloodshed in Northern Ireland must distinguish between the pre-Internment and post-Internment periods. Pre-Internment effects upon the Irish in Britain were to be perceived at various levels. Among the 'politicized', i.e., those members of the previously-listed organizations, the routine of meetings continued with be-flagged and ragged processions of Irish protesters almost every weekend in London and Birmingham. Fleet Street newspaper editors became resigned to extra mail deliveries of irate letters from correspondents with Irish-sounding names, proposing a wide variety of conflicting solutions. In 'Irish' pubs and clubs, collections for the I.R.A. met with generous response. Bernadette Devlin, though pregnant with impending out-of-wedlock child, was fêted at meetings, and, remembering Parnell, that reaction at least marked a departure from traditional attitudes.

Traditional attitudes, however, were maintained by the petty bickering that existed between the various organizations. The introduction of Internment by the Ulster Government on 13 August, 1971—incurring detention of hundreds of 'suspects' —and the scope of the backlash provided the émigré organizations with some measure of agreement. The subsequent formation of the Anti-Internment League in Britain allowed many of the bodies at least to co-operate in being united against the Internment measures. Internment also produced another side-effect of minor interest. Student opinion at English universities became polarized along the lines of the Suez differences of 1956. At one of the largest immigrant demonstrations in 1971 it was notable that half the marchers were made up of contingents of International Socialists from the various universities, forming a rare alliance of British intelligentsia and immigrant

Irish, and providing a hark–back to the demonstrations of the 1920s in protest against Government policy in Ireland at the time.

A more dramatic hark–back to the twenties was an explosion in London on the morning of the march, 31 October, when a charge of plastic blasted a floor of the prestige 600 ft Post Office Tower and sent tons of masonry and steel tumbling through the early–morning quietude of Central London. The following day's newspapers were unanimous in assuming I.R.A. responsibility; an assumption encouraged by the anonymous joker who rang the Press Association and declared the explosion to be 'the work of the Kilburn (London) battalion of the I.R.A.'. Curiously enough, none of the known members of the I.R.A. who stewarded the march later that day were questioned by the authorities. Nevertheless, the incident incurred a week of scare–mongering and unearthed the inevitable crop of hoaxers.

The Irish community generally reacted to the explosion in terms of neighbours' reactions – which were tolerant. That good natured tolerance was to severely diminish during the months following Internment, directly affected by the deaths of British soldiers in Ulster. The Internment policy of the Ulster Government, which had been successful in the twenties, thirties, and fifties in containing 'the enemy within the gates', now produced running gun–battles on the streets of Belfast. Following the fateful 13 August 1971, each successive week witnessed the death of a soldier in Ulster and a consequent hardening of attitude in Britain towards 'the Oirish'. There was no overt antagonism on the scale of the 1920s; rather a series of isolated instances: The State Theatre in London's Kilburn, an area of heavy Irish concentration, refused to accept the traditional St Patrick's Day Concert for 1972. The theatre owners, the Rank Organization, claimed bomb–threat fears and other political considerations. English Catholic parishioners complained to their priests concerning collections outside church doors for Republican funds. A Tipperary–born priest, Father Michael Connolly, serving in a Wolverhampton parish, was taken to task by Enoch Powell M.P., over a newspaper report of remarks allegedly made by the priest at an I.R.A. meeting in Dublin. In South London, an Irishwoman who had collected for Ulster refugees in 1970 (her neighbours had generously donated) received in this soldier–killing latter half of 1971 a predictably hostile reaction from neighbours.

Stronger reaction was provoked by the events in Londonderry of January 1972, when soldiers of the Parachute Brigade advanced into the Bogside area of the city—held by the I.R.A. —and thirteen civilians died under fire. In the ensuing spate of charge and counter-charge, British hostility towards the Irish reached a new pitch; the Irish generally believing the civilians to have been murdered while most of the British public remained convinced that the soldiers had first been fired upon.

For the Irish, all the inherited ghostly victims of history were revived in emotional hysteria, culminating with the burning of the British Embassy in Dublin ... which produced a backlash of hostility towards the immigrants in Britain. Offices of Irish businesses were inundated with telephonic exhortations to 'go home, Paddy' and at more vulnerable levels of employment, Irish secretaries and white-collar workers faced sudden refusals of employment. This hostility was heightened some weeks later when an I.R.A. retaliatory explosion at the Aldershot, Hampshire barracks of the Parachute Brigade snuffed out the lives, not of soldiers, but of five women cleaners, a priest and a gardener. The explosion, comparable to the Fenian dynamiting of Clerkenwell Prison which had claimed a dozen innocent lives a century previous, left a residue of hostility likely to linger for some time.

An immediate reaction to the Aldershot deaths was a slump in demand for branded Irish goods, with one supermarket chain in London clearing its shelves of Irish produce, while in the Midlands a large accountancy firm instructed its branches to divest themselves of Irish clients. There were some sporadic incidents in public houses and in one such flare–up in the Holloway district of London knives were used in a running fracas between Irish and West Indian protagonists. In Luton, a town with a substantial Irish population, a man collecting for the dependents of internees in Northern Ireland had his garage set on fire.

These were some of the outward manifestations of an impatient British public, increasingly affected by the murderous turn of events in Ulster. At a less dramatic level there followed strained business and personal relations between elements of both communities; the most common outlet being to switch off the television or radio news when visitors were present. That way at least, some painful discussions were avoided, and not least within the Irish community itself, for whom the Ulster escalation proved divisive. A million people, albeit Irish, cannot live by–and–large contentedly in Britain without feeling some degree of loyalty for the ways and mores of that country. Thus the Irish Guards regiment of the British Army, for instance, have since the 1900s drawn heavily from among the Irish in Britain – and it would be a foolhardy accuser who would speculate on their loyalty to Queen and Country.

All through the Ulster troubles, Irishmen served in the British Army in Northern Ireland. Some such indeed were killed or wounded. The overriding divisiveness, however, lay with the ingrained attitude of the Irish community, which found itself in the nebulous position of desiring the withdrawal of a British military presence in Ireland while at the same time being grateful to benefit from the variegated offerings of life in Britain. Put another way, the Irish in Britain are happy to avail themselves of the advanced social welfare system which—to extend the logic of nationalistic political sympathies—they would deny their compatriots in Northern Ireland. When it comes to extreme political agitation, it is a contradiction which most are not unaware of.

The fact that such a small proportion actively engage in agitation about the Ulster situation is another telling commentary on the extent to which the Irish, as a community, have become absorbed into the British spectrum in recent years. They are loathe to put at risk their prime concern of day–to–day living; indeed for the majority the word 'politician' does not evoke any meaningful response. As Eamonn McCann, left–wing revolutionary and friend of Bernadette Devlin, says: 'There is no horde of proletarian Irish ... ready and waiting to pour out from Camden Town, Cricklewood and Kilburn to stop the heart of Empire. They are too worried about the rent rises announced last month by the Greater London Council.'

And that, really, is the nub of the matter and death–knell

of appreciable political radicalism among the immigrants. What have the million or so Irish in Britain to be radical about, when all their civil, religious, and social rights are given to them? and in a 'foreign' country: more rights indeed than most of them could hope for in the 'Ould Ireland' of Saturday night chanting nostalgia. For the majority of that million Irish in Britain have bitter–black memories of their materially in-opportune youth in Ireland and of the failure of the Republic to provide them with the glories so fiercely promised by the visionary creators of that state in 1916. As one weary agitator remarked: 'All they're good for now is cursing the English on Saturday night with their free National Health teeth.'

'... National Health teeth' is relevant. The unlikely spectacle of a million Irish in Britain demanding with one voice the immediate withdrawal of Britain from Northern Ireland would be a supreme irony – given that that community eagerly and gratefully accept the benefits of the British Welfare struc-ture here. (As a pertinent aside, the Irish in Britain in 1970 had access to social services costing £170 per head of population, whereas the comparative figure for the Irish Republic was £68 per person.)

The writer Claud Cockburn put it another way, in his column in the *Irish Times*. They were, he said, 'more interested in proving themselves a cut above the Pakistani'. And that too has relevance, for most remember the 'No Irish' signs of the forties and fifties. The pressures of history dictate that they be cautious and conservative. Any guilt-feelings they may have about 'Ould Ireland' can be quickly allayed by a trip home and the dramatic contrast between the range of opportunities available to them in their own homeland compared with those available in Britain. The economic base underlying post–famine immigration is an all-powerful one. The mass of the Irish in Britain are content with their lives here: many indeed find their situation to be one of rewarding challenge and achieve-ment. Only a tiny proportion of those settled—around five thousand—return in any one year. The remainder have neither time nor temperament for headline heroics, but have instead the private heroism of having pulled themselves up by their boot-straps. They of 'the middle nation' embody the tenet that the first responsibility of the Irish in Britain is to the Irish in Britain. They are, by and large, on good terms with their neighbours and reasonably well adjusted to their adopted environment. Their children will grow up to become the 'Brit–Irish' with mixed feelings. They have no desire to fly a tricolour over Camden Town, and though they pay ritual lip-service to flying one over Belfast they will not do much to aid that fluttering. When it comes to political radicalism, the Irish in Britain react with the unspoken awareness of a more personal corollary: that of their own communal struggle in overcoming the material disadvantages of being born in Ireland and the patently lesser disadvantages of living now in Britain. That they may go unhindered about that effort is to them sufficient 'radicalism' to the day.

7

In Business

If the sixties were notable for the improvement of the immigrants' living standards, and of their developing and participating in the political mainstream, it was also the decade which saw their increasing involvement in business. As their involvement with the Labour party sprang essentially from grass–roots identification with the personality of that party, so did their emergence in business reflect their own grass–roots activity in two industries, building and drink.

They had, since the Great Famine exodus of the mid–nineteenth century, been prominent in construction trades as navvies and workmen. By the turn of the century the tradition had become so well established that the hardy men of the Irish western seaboard—and most other rural areas—had little thought for any other kind of work upon arrival in Britain. Indeed their Irish adolescence was filled with tales and jargon of English building sites, of 'shuttering' and 'four by two's', of jigs and joists and cranes and all the technical paraphernalia of the building site. Every Irish schoolboy knows the popular parody of answer to the Penny Catechism question which asks:

> Who made the World?
> McAlpine,* sir!

Most Irish adolescents know too, of the legendary 'big money' to be made in the building sites, Inevitably, the Irish who spent most of their working lives digging down and building up in Britain bequeathed some expertise to their children, so that by the 1930s many small construction firms were owned by first–

---

* McAlpine: A well-known British construction firm.

121

generation Irish. The occasional family effort blossomed into larger–scale enterprise, such as Gleeson's, but by and large most firms of Irish origin remained medium–sized until the building boom which followed the Second World War. It was this post-war expansion which opened the hard–graft path to development and riches. Vast reaches of cities needed to be rebuilt, new towns and housing estates were on the drawing–boards of every major local authority in the country. The one group ready and eager to rebuild Britain were the Irish. In the London–Irish dance halls of the Blitz a cheer would sometimes break out upon the fall of a nearby bomb, not for any reason of racial animosity, but rather for the prospect of building work on the morrow. One man who has a vivid recollection of that period (and who prefers to remain anonymous) came to the Midlands as a raw adolescent from the west of Ireland. He took up trade as a plasterer, slept two to a bed in homely digs: 'If you weren't up by an early hour, the landlady got you up. I've seen grown men having their bare arses slapped.' He scrupulously attended his religious duties, hunted among compatriots for a copy of 'The Western' (*Western People*, his home-town newspaper) and hit for London and acres of plastering in the post–war building boom.

In London he settled in digs near Camden Town, was offered more work than he could cope with and took on a friend. Even then he could not plaster all he was offered so he contracted–out to another. Today, twenty-five years later, he presides over a multiplicity of construction interests, with an annual turnover of millions, and has belatedly time to indulge in the cultural interests which he denied himself in the helter–skelter of fortune building. His story has been repeated, to a varying degree, among many others of the Irish builders who came to 'dig for gold in the streets'. Their prime attribute was hard work, allied to that ambition common to émigrés the world over, namely the desire to have some achievement or material wealth as reward for the very act of exile. With the predominance of the Irish in the building industry, the very fact of being Irish was, of course, in itself an advantage, a factor which applied particularly to the rural Irish, who are more dour, insular and unco-operative with outsiders.

The Irish have become so influential in the building industry that on certain big money jobs it's not sufficent merely to be Irish to get work. In certain areas, one must come from a particular county in Ireland! Sections of the Victoria Line—London's latest underground artery which travels under the Thames—were built by teams of Donegal men who jealously guarded the big earnings for themselves. (One of their games, when bored, was to find who could toss a bag of cement farthest.)

Certainly for the entrepreneural–minded Irishman, the ability to handle and lead his own countrymen was a necessary ingredient of the rise to forming his own company. Often he was helped by his brothers, for in that hierarchy of family maleness, lay, in effect, the sort of sophisticated management structure that I.B.M. and I.C.I. try so expensively to maintain. At its most basic, the advantage of a group of brothers forming a company was that it would take a very brave man indeed to 'cross' them on a deal: in the early days of a new company's life the reputation of a group of brothers stood them in good stead when a challenge—often physical—arose from some quarter or other.

Hardly surprising, then, to note that the six leading Irish construction companies in Britain are all commanded by brothers; brothers who in most cases have come up through the ranks together, having started their working lives by digging down and staying on to build up business empires. The flair, panache, and toughness of these brotherly enterprises have given rise to many legends within the Irish community, such as the Irish contractor whose tender to construct the 'Chunnel'—the projected tunnel under the English Channel to France—was so low in price that he was called in by the Government officers to elaborate. The contractor explained the low tender on the grounds that his business was a family one: his brother would start tunnelling from Dover while he himself would start at Calais, and they would meet in the middle of the Channel. 'But supposing you don't meet?' he was asked. 'Ah, well then, we'll give ye two tunnels for the price of one.'

Similar stories contribute to the mystique of how fortunes were made and construction groups fashioned by lowly labourers from rural Ireland. Of how a large plant–hire firm

owes its origins to the morning when two brothers took leave of
a building site—in the company of a hoist. And of how that
hoist and a few picks and drills which had been 'collected' from
the building site, were later seen in a yard over which hung the
proud family inscription of the brothers' names as plant–hire
providers. And of how, ten years later, the two enterprising
brothers now preside over a group whose annual plant investment runs at half a million.

These are the stories that Irish labourers like to tell as they
quench the drought of a hard day's graft. The implication being
that perhaps one of these days they themselves will take the
first plunge into sub-contracting, after which there will be no
looking back, but only forward to Jaguar cars and drawing-
board chat and the big house in London's Highgate (up the
hill from Camden Town).

Underneath such romanticism, however, lies the hard graft
of effort. None of the Irish construction firms were built up on
an eight-hour day, but rather on long hours, every day of the
week. And to the detriment, in personality terms, of many of
the founders of these companies. The narrow concentration
upon the mechanics of building, the long hours, the incessant
travel, and the near–total immersion of energy in the business
has left many of these men materially wealthy but culturally
impoverished. Some, wisely, perceive the signs of personality
disintegration and hand over control to a son, or to colleagues.
Others cling on, in spite of all medical or family advice to the
contrary, for their companies are their lives' work and often the
only real 'thing' in their lives, the prop-up of vanity and of their
very personalities. For them, work takes the lion's share of
their energies, leaving them as powerful builders of motorways
and housing estates and, by the same token, painfully inadequate in many other areas of social and cultural activity.

Take, as example, the progression of a young man from insular rural Ireland, who left school at thirteen, takes the emigrant
boat at fifteen, becomes a ganger on a London building site at
twenty-one, a partner in a small sub–contracting firm at
twenty-five, and a wealthy man in his forties; who by sheer
dint of experience and toughness finishes housing estates within
penalty–clause schedule. That man may never have the motiva-

tion to read one book (except a thriller) or realize his potential in other areas of his personality. The desire to 'get on', the later success in doing so, and the subsequent demands of consolidating that success leave many such successful builders bereft of fulfilment in the 'cultural' areas of their personality.

This is not to take a churlish view of their otherwise impressive achievements, but rather to recognize the penalties exacted by the rigours of their life's effort. Certainly the men who came to prominence in the sixties are more aware of the world about them than their predecessors: one heartening change, for instance, has been the extent to which some successful Irish businessmen have recently involved themselves in the welfare of their less well-off compatriots. Increasingly in recent years have a handful of businessmen contributed to the expansion of social welfare services among the Irish community, to helping with time, talent, and money towards the expansion of Irish centres throughout Britain. At a more individual level there is one dramatic example known to this writer of a man who founded and master-minded a construction firm to the expansion of a multi-million corporation, who in his forties went to university and gained a business degree with speed. Partially, no doubt, to be conversant with the management language of his college-trained executives, but also to prove happily he could do it.

The company he had helped build in Britain—Abbey Homesteads—was left in the care of his younger brother, Charles Gallagher. Under the latter's entrepreneural guidance the company by 1971 had an annual turnover of £5,000,000, its seven hundred employees had accounted for 20,000 new homes and it had built housing estates in Cyprus. Charles Gallagher himself is a powerful and benevolent figure among the Irish community in London and currently superintending the expansion of the Irish Centre in Camden Town.

At a similar level of business and community impact is Tony Beatty, an accountant by profession and a tycoon by instinct. With a background of the typical immigrant coming from rural Ireland, Beatty slogged nights to gain his accountancy qualifications, built up clients among the Irish immigrant building community, founded his own consultancy, and is now the wealthy director of many concerns including a merchant bank. Much of his initial business activity was among the Irish; financial, taxation and accountancy advice to small and medium-sized builders. Latterly he has expanded his business interests to include catering, car-hire, travel and holidays. His invest-ments and clients are now about equally divided between Irish and British. Nevertheless, the original strain of Irish–based activity continues, most significantly with the immigrants' weekly newspaper, the *Irish Post*, which he founded in 1970 and which now enjoys a weekly circulation of thirty thousand copies, heavily supported with advertising from Irish-run public houses. Its impact upon the Irish in Britain has been profound, not least in its reflection of that community to itself. The significance of entrepreneurs such as Charles Gallagher, Tony Beatty, and others is that, having made their pile, so to speak, they remain involved in the welfare at large of the émigré community which has, in a sense, produced them. Not the least contributory influence upon the upgrading of that community during the sixties has been the effective interest of part of the Irish business community in providing material help and advice.

The dual business success of the Irish in building and public house management—and its reference to the community—may be best seen in the expansion of the Irish Centres in the major towns and cities. These centres provide a much needed meeting and recreation ground for the mainly rural immigrants and have attached to them trained social workers who perform a multitude of tasks to ease the culture shock of the more inadequate in transferring from a warm social life in Ireland to the more impersonal hurly–burly existence in a British city.

The expansion of these centres in the sixties was con-siderably aided by Irish builders who fulfilled the building requirements at a marginal profit (or at cost) and by British brewing companies who advanced the necessary funds in return for the monopoly contract as drink suppliers to the centres. That the breweries should thus so confidently loan substantial amounts of money to one ethnic group is explained by their confidence in that ethnic group as consumers and purveyors of their products. It comes as no surprise, somehow, to learn that half the eight thousand public houses in the London area are managed or controlled by Irish-men. Like the construction industry, their success in this field is due to a combination of tradition, flair, and essentially hard work.

There is also the critical factor of being master in their own house which appeals so strongly to the Irish as a race. It is the ambition of most young Irish barmen to gain control of their own premises, which most duly do, having served time with two 'guv'nors' and been recommended by them to a brewery for tenancy.

All businesses have their 'dishonesties'. The construction and drink trades are no exception. Underpinning the émigré success in both are two sensitive areas, needful of comment. In the building trade it is the practice known as 'lumping': in the pub business, the fiddle is known as 'buying outside'.

'The lump' refers to sub-contracted labour which is paid by the hour or day and is neither insured, registered, nor officially recorded. This, briefly, is how it operates. Take the case of a large contract, where a variety of jobs will be sub–contracted by the main contractor: site excavation, clearance, foundations, services, walls, floors, ceilings, etc. These will be sub–contracted to smaller firms who will employ additional labour. This additional casual labour will be paid at a daily rate, the rate varying according to the skill. Where 'the lump' oper-ates, the daily rate is paid without the deduction of income tax or insurance. The sub–contractor has gained the contract on a fixed sum. Where he can make excess profit is in the difference between the amount *claimed* for labour and what he *actually pays his labour*. I understand the addition of fictitious names was, until recently, commonplace. A sub–contractor would in-clude in his tender say, thirty men at £8 per day for twenty days to complete the specified work. In reality he would employ, say, twenty–five men thereby ensuring himself an immediate excess profit. It was almost impossible to challenge his figures, as no precise records of names and insurance details were kept.

Undoubtedly many contractors and sub-contractors grew rapidly rich on 'the lump'. Undoubtedly, too, the system was not confined to the Irish, though temperamentally it suited them well, offering the advantages of tax–free earnings

and freedom from irksome officialdom. The system appealed,
too, to the Irish labourer's desire to be a free agent and to work
and travel at will. 'The lump' provided him with good money
for hard work and no bother from the English tax man! It
solidified his sense of being in Britain for a short time and
nurtured the illusion of 'going home next year'. The disadvantages were, of course, that most often he did not 'go home
next year' but stayed on for most of his adult life. The penalties
of such fond illusion, and of 'the lump', were brought sharply
home if he fell ill or was injured. Then, for all his years' hard
labour and easy money, there were no welfare benefits. I recall
the middle–aged Irishman with whom I regularly played darts
in a North London pub. One evening blood seeped from his leg
to the pub–floor. I helped him to the toilet where he dripped
blood into the bowl from a broken vein, and tied a tourniquet.
He refused to be helped to a nearby hospital, on the grounds
that 'they would only want me name and address'. He had lived
fifteen years in Britain, worked mainly on the building sites
under 'the lump' and was terrified of bureaucracy. Probably a
proportion of those high earnings had been faithfully remitted
to a family in Ireland, but now in his middle–age he had little
to show for the years except a single room, his game of darts,
and fear of the authorities. He was a simple, civilized man.
There are thousands like him among the Irish in Britain upon
whose bent and labouring backs many an Irish fortune has been
built.

For better or worse, that system is rapidly declining: April
1972 sounded the death–knell of 'the lump', officially at least.
From that date all building labour was required to be
scrupulously registered, and though some Irish contractors will
mourn the demise of 'the lump', the majority will adjust to
the change for they have, in the sixties, become more adjusted
to the permanence of their stay in Britain.

Those grown rich upon the system are now mostly 'respectable' and eager to be accepted as such. For whatever its de-
merits, 'the lump' did allow the immigrant Irish to gain a
foothold and consolidate their claim upon an environment
which, literally, they helped to build. Criticisms of the Irish
labour force in the construction industry most often centre

about their capacity to skimp bureaucracy—they work under false names and pay no Income Tax—but the criticisms ignore the fact that such omissions are not confined to the Irish. Indeed such practices grew up with the industry—as did the Irish—but the habits of evasion were rife long before the Irish became prominent.

Perhaps the best example of the decline of 'the lump' are the hundreds of thousands of building workers who, this year, will be registered under the tax category of 'Schedule D', for the self-employed. Hand–in–hand with the current decline in 'the lump' is the increase in Irish–owned construction firms and interests, and more significantly, the growing number of Irish executives in the large British building corporations such as Wimpey and Laing. They have, in a sense, come over 'the lump', of early labouring, of being 'hewers of wood and drawers of water', and progressed to being an integrated and potent force in the construction industry.

OF PUBS AND PUBLICANS

In the area of drink and public houses, their rise has been, if anything, more dramatic and again most clearly seen in the sixties. It was predictable, perhaps, that they should make such an impact upon that area of leisure, given the traditional sacred place of the pub in native Irish society. In the rural towns and villages from which most immigrants came, the pub is the natural business and social centre, the latter–day equivalent of the Roman Forum, wherein the day–to–day business of the community is transacted. On par with the priest, the publican is the most influential figure, and the respository of as many secrets. (During two lengthy strikes by banking–staff in Ireland during the sixties, the pubs assumed the function of cashing cheques and advancing capital. Local publicans held as shrewd and informed knowledge of a client's credit–worthiness as did a bank manager.)

The demerit was, and is, the stagnant decay of the rural reaches, where little prospect of succession to such tribal power is offered to the rising generations. The young men who take the emigrant boat to England, thus conditioned by the pubautocracy of their background, soon find a natural vocational outlet in dispensing alcoholic refreshment to the cosmopolitan clientele of British cities. Often, of course, they find their first serving stint in an Irish house where the bulk of the custom is Irish. The novice's capacity for handling the vagaries of his own people in the often tumultuous atmosphere of Irish pubs in Britain provides an early teething in pub (and people) management. The good order of many an 'Irish' public house is maintained not only by the understandable ability of the landlord to speak the language of his clientele, but also on occasion by his physical courage in quietening a punch-up. Consequently, the encouragement to Irish personnel by the various large and powerful British breweries is not due to any ethnic benevolence, but rather to the experienced assessment that the Irish, on the whole, make pretty competent tenants and managers. They work long and arduously, as demanded by the nature of the business, but having additionally the motive, common to many immigrant groups, of wishing to succeed. Thus most take an inordinate pride in the running of their houses and in imparting the classical bonhomie of the host. Many, also, make the much sought fortune, through a combination of hard work and good sense, flair, and 'buying outside'.

BUYING OUTSIDE

The majority of the 72,000 public houses in Britain are owned by breweries and are known as 'tied houses', i.e. the beer sold comes from the brewery owner. Most pubs are run by tenants or managers; the manager is on a fixed salary with a possible share of the profits, while the tenant, by contrast, formally buys his beer, wines and spirits from the brewery and all the profits ensuing from subsequent sales are his. The tenant personally bears the cost of upkeeping and furnishing the premises, the salaries of staff and improvement; all, of course, geared to increased consumption and profits. Thus a tenant who combines flair with application may substantially increase his turnover of alcohol to a level which provides him, personally, with a substantial income. (A personal income of around £5,000 a year is not uncommon from a house of busy trade.)

Where extra profit may be accrued is through the practice of 'buying outside', by which the tenant, having increased beer sales to a level satisfactory to the owning brewery, then purchases additional stock from another supplier at rates more profitable to himself.

Hardly surprising, then, that most émigré Irish prefer the tenancy of a house, and will often bid large sums—from £3,000 upwards—to secure the tenancy of a 'good' house. Family feeling operates considerably here, in that a successful elder brother will often recommend his younger brother for a tenancy, and provide the necessary initial finance to get him started. Often, too, the bulk of local trade will be Irish, extending to social and sporting clubs using the premises regularly for meetings and business. There is also the interaction of construction, public house and community interests: an Irishman, having accrued capital through a building interest, will often invest that capital in purchasing a pub tenancy and at some later date help set up a former workmate as publican. Equally his premises will be available for a benefit dance to raise funds for the family of a former workmate killed or injured on a building site.

As the practice of 'lumping' grew up with the construction industry, so did the system of 'buying outside' develop with the licensed trade. In recent years, however, the benign tolerance of the breweries to such practice has somewhat diminished. At least one of the major brewers now increasingly prefers to install managers rather than tenants.

As the sixties witnessed the developing influence of the Irish at management levels of the construction industry, so were the Irish–run public houses improving their décor and facilities and the general quality of their premises, without, for the most part, turning their backs on the bulk of hard–drinking trade. Thus in many Irish-run public houses the labourers from a nearby building-site feel free to inhabit the carpeted lounge bar after work, knowing themselves to be a valued part of an ethnic trade. Similarly Saturday night in the areas of say, Camden or Kentish Town in London, or Sparkbrook in Birmingham is awash with alcoholic nostalgia for things Irish. And though the décor and carpeting may be new, the plaintive songs are nineteenth–

century indulgences, badly crooned, in the main, against an atmosphere of cigarette smog and sullen faces. (Whatever the other diverse effects of emigration from Ireland, the 'typically Irish' pub of a Saturday night is, to this writer at least, depressing. Gathered into smoky congress, subject to an unceasing din of spurious nostalgia, the former inhabitants of rural towns and villages in Ireland summon to mind the ghettoism of the 'coffin-ships' of enforced migration. The stray English visitor on a Saturday night in North London may wonder if he is still in England as he vainly searches for a quiet 'English' pub in the outer reaches of Islington or Hammersmith.)

If the Irish in London are thus prominent in the pub trade, they are less so in the provinces. In the southern counties they are to be found in farming, market-gardening, and racehorse training. (One of the Queen Mother's two horse trainers is an Irishman.) In the west Midlands they are prominent as managers of supermarkets. In the Midlands, a chain of dry-cleaning shops is Irish-owned; at white collar level generally there is a sprinkling in banking and insurance. But in the mainstream of big business, there is but tiny Irish representation. In the Stock Exchange and in the upper managerial echelons of finance groups and large corporations Irish representation is minute, certainly by contrast with, say, Jewish representation. It could, of course, be argued that democratic British representation in these areas is equally low; the Stock Exchange for instance, being mainly a warren of family and public school connections. The obvious cause of lack of Irish impact in these areas is one of tradition – the Ireland which produced the mass of the Irish in Britain was under-industralized and consequently unable to provide the training and skills required in these areas. (The sixties brought some improvement: the Gross National Product in Ireland in that decade rose by 125 per cent and the average annual industrial growth was 7 per cent.)

The decade also saw the establishment of 500 new industrial projects with attendant training (often abroad) in new industrial skills for a generation of Irish in Ireland. This new industrialization was perceptible among the recent immigrants to Britain, most dramatically in the new breed of Irish executives, of whom

Tony O'Reilly is a prime example. O'Reilly, a former Rugby International, moved from Ireland to Britain in 1969, but hardly as a traditional immigrant. He came rather as Managing Director of Heinz, U.K., the British section of the multi–million foods corporation. And when he arrived in a chauffeur–driven limousine to turn out for the local London–Irish rugger team at suburban matches, the image of the traditional Irish immigrant took a severe knocking.

O'Reilly is a product of the industrial boom of the early sixties in Ireland, and the consequent adaption to new managerial skills – with relevant effects upon immigrants to Britain. The growth of an Irish employment agency in London, Emerald Staff Agency, mirrors this improvement. When the agency began in 1959, it specialized in placing Irish workers in the catering and hotel trade. Ten years later, it had spouted branch offices in predictable parts of London – Hammersmith, Shepherds Bush, Clapham – and broadened the variety of skills on offer to British firms, in response to the more skilled quality of immigrants from Ireland. A measure of this improved quality was demonstrated in 1970 when the Emerald Agency supplied over a hundred computer personnel direct from Ireland to help staff a giant computer complex of the National West-minster Bank in London. Ten years earlier that numerical strength of skills would simply have been non–existent in Ireland; a time when factory managers on a Croydon industrial estate complained that Irish workers were incompetent and fumbling in dealing with precision assembly work.

An equally significant pointer to this changing reality was the entry of a leading Irish banking combine into the British market, depending initially on the increased affluence of the immigrants. Allied Irish Banks in 1970 established a full banking service to the general public in the dominantly-Irish district of Kilburn in London; almost every Irishman of financial substance in the half-million strong London-Irish community was present at the dinner to celebrate the bank's opening venture into the British market. The bank's hospitality and pre–launch intelligence operation was amply rewarded in subsequent months when it gathered in £1,000,000 worth of accounts, most of which came from the Irish community, being personal and business accounts. A third of the customers were non-Irish. One year after opening, the branch held accounts totalling £2,000,000 and received an accolade normally reserved for branches of the Big Five (British) banks, that of being raided by gangsters. Allied Irish now have six banking branches in Britain, almost all centred upon areas of strong Irish communities, but with the clientele being about one third non-Irish and the projection indicating a levelling–off at around half–and–half Irish-British clients. From the point of view of business expansion, the slogan may well be: 'First find your ethnic market'. With a million Irish–born in Britain, this is a philosophy being further investigated by Irish–based manufacturers eager to gain a foothold on the wider U.K. market. The sixties saw this ethnic market being tapped by Irish manufacturers of cigarettes, confectionery, and foodstuffs who through the advertising medium of the *Irish Post* newspaper sustained a consumer impact upon the ethnic market as a base from which to expand into the wider U.K. market.

A brief look at the history of the consumer-drink, Guinness, provides a pointer to the possibilities of the ethnic market. First brewed in Dublin in 1759, the drink was supplied from there to a growing British market for almost two hundred years. Being in the nature of a national drink in Ireland, its increased consumption in Britain initially rested on the loyalty of Irish immigrants who helped make it popular among the working-classes generally: it was not until 1936 that its consumption in Britain required the establishment of a brewery here. Today, when Guinness is a name in the 130 countries of foreign export, the company preserves its contact with the Irish. In Dublin the company is the largest private employer of labour and in terms of staff relations and welfare schemes sets a lead for every other Irish concern. It also donates substantial annual amounts to charities. Among the Irish in Britain, the company keeps equally strong and benevolent links, generously supports socio–cultural events in the community and has, for instance, underwritten the substantial overdraft of the Irish Club in London's Eaton Square.

In the reverse direction, the talents of successful businessmen from among the Irish in Britain have been channelled back to Ireland, through the London–based lobbying of the Industrial Development Authority (a body sponsored by the Irish Government) which informs entrepreneurs of industrial development opportunities in Ireland and provides substantial grants towards the initiation of new industries, particularly in the areas most depleted through emigration.

Each successive year of the sixties has witnessed an increase in such return investment of finance and skills – a measure of the growth of the Irish business community in Britain. There is also evidence of a substantially increased return of finance to Irish banking institutions, principally investment and deposit account renderings which qualify for the tax–free non–residential accumulation of interest. It may be remarked, however, that the newly–acquired affluence of the community during the last decade has not been proportionately matched by contributions from the business sector towards the welfare of the community generally: the 'community sense' of individuals noted earlier being characteristic of but a minority of the business sector. This lack of community cohesion is most noticeable in the area of social problems such as adolescent delinquency, alcoholism, and general inadequacy where the major activity of prevention and rehabilitation rests substantially with the combined efforts of British statutory agencies and Catholic Church interests – the contribution from the business community being extremely meagre. This paucity of effort from the newly affluent occasioned one priest, prominent in the London–Irish community, to remark that affluence was 'producing a breed of vulgar, materialistic savages. God help Ireland when she becomes prosperous, if this is how we behave when we get some money.' Another observer remarked that 'we're breeding a race of Irish Jews over here', with unconscious contradiction, for the self-help of British Jewry startlingly highlights the absence of similar organized welfare among the Irish. It may well be, of course, that the various racial persecutions of the Jews has left them with a more concerted awareness of the need for self–help than the Irish, though a visit to any Irish club with its relentless décor of green shamrocks would appear to belie that easy explanation. The more likely explanation for lack of Irish welfare cohesion may reside in a combination of factors; the fact that growth of the business sector, while being substantial, is comparatively recent; and the fact that for many there is still a residual indecision of identity, an ambivalance as to fully accepting Britain as 'home', occasioned by obvious historical pressures and the proximity of Ireland.

Nevertheless, some of the changes of the past decade indicate that this 'crisis of identity' is being resolved, at least in the attitude of some pioneering individuals towards efforts of community self–help, and notably in the activities of the *Irish Post* which has raised several trust–funds from among its readers to ensure the material well–being of families hit by misfortune.

But the weighty spectrum of the professional and business community, by contrast to such isolated endeavours, is characterized by a distinct absence of community awareness —while containing in its recent growth the potential to considerably aid the well-being not only of the Irish in Britain, but in Ireland. The annual remittance to relatives in Ireland of over £10,000,000 from among the 'ordinary' Irish immigrants is but an indication of the resources available in the professional-business sector of the community.

Whether this potential can be effectively harnessed is a matter of potentially radical influence upon the entire pattern of Irish immigration, and a matter of immediate import for those immigrants who inhabit that twilight area of what is politely called 'social problems'.

8

With some 'Social Problems'

Between 1950 and 1960, the contribution of the Irish to violent crime in London rose from 9.7 per cent to 12.2 per cent —yet they formed only 2 to 3 per cent of the population of the metropolis.[19]

In the same decade, Irish–born from the Republic accounted for 12 per cent of the prison population of England, Scotland, and Wales—yet only 2 per cent of the total population were Irish born.

In 1966, a study undertaken in Birmingham demonstrated that the Irish were responsible for: 23 per cent of violent crime; 20 per cent of property offences; 17 per cent of offences of prostitution; 60 per cent of offences of drunkenness. Yet Irish-born formed but 7 per cent of the population of the area studied.[20]

These excerpts summarize what to many native British is the 'Irish Question', i.e. the presence of an immigrant community with a capacity for drunkenness, fighting, and court appearances. Much of the Irish over-representation in the various criminal studies of the past ten years is indeed due to a combination of drunkenness and domestic dispute, allied to the propensity to 'let fly' at a protagonist. Fist–fighting is a strong cultural strain in the Irish, not generally regarded as offensive, even in middle-class ethos; by and large tolerated and, on occasions, admired. (By no means all Irish fights are as sporting as the Irish them–selves would like to believe. I have seen many vicious fights in Irish pubs, with bottles and boots liberally used. The knife, however, is usually alien to an all–Irish fight.)

But given the propensity for 'clouting' and for inebriation, the Irish in Britain appear disproportionately prominent in crime statistics. Being dismissive of that oft–quoted comment on statistics—'there are three kinds of lies: lies, damned lies, and statistics'—and looking rather to the hidden variables pertaining to the above comparisons, one finds that the very composition of the Irish émigré grouping makes them prone to a high appearance in law–breaking statistics. (1) Most crime is committed by males between fifteen and forty–four, in which groups there are disproportionately high numbers of Irish, compared to the native population. (2) The Irish are over-represented among the urban poor, and among the inhabitants of decaying city areas where the crime rate, anyway, is high.

There is also the critical element of 'culture–shock', the effects upon the personality of moving from one community to another. As the author of the Birmingham report, John Lambert, says:

> Release from the stringent controls of the home society pro-vokes something of a reaction which finds expression in relatively greater crime and disorder, theft, and drunkenness – the expression of those for whom immigration has not brought economic security, stable family relations, and other signs of success in this new country.

The culture–shock of transference undoubtedly accounts for a good deal of criminality, particularly at the level of petty thievery and drunkenness among adolescents who in Ireland would have less opportunity for such indulgence. At its simplest, parental influence is sufficient to inhibit such activities. The absence of family influence is perhaps the first culture–shock awareness of adolescent immigrants. At a deeper, and perhaps more meaningful level, the very act of transference from one contrasting environment to another can induce detrimental personality effects. At its most superficial, the departure from a close tribal society, heavily laden (and propped up) with myth and superstition induces a feeling of nakedness and vulnerability. The new environment initially presents problems, not least of language and manners. The expressions 'please' and 'thank you', for instance are much more widely used in English society, at all levels, than in Ireland. And the fact that all Irish immigrants speak English is of little help: the assumption from the host society being that because the Irish speak English, then they should have English manners. Similarly, the myths of Irish history hang in the brain of many an Irishman, who expects the English to measure–up to the awe–inspiring imperial caricatures of his nationalistic Irish education, and is somewhat thrown to find instead a rather disinterested, polite, and self–sufficient people. The English in turn may express some disillusion if the Irishman be found to be abstemious, or dull or unable to sing! (It may surprise English readers to know that Ireland, on the whole, contains a higher proportion of teetotal adults than Britain. Equally, readers in Ireland should know that many Englishmen care not a fig for the lost Empire and are, in fact, rather glad to be rid of it.) Relations between the races are thus inhibited and thrown lopsided by the weight of mutually inherited myths, to the extent that, by and large, both races prefer the company of their own and can mix better with other nationalities, than with each other.

New immigrants, while being curious about the English, are also often highly sensitive to the real or imagined differences. A common initial reaction among new immigrant Irish is that of interpreting the routine curtness of metropolitan shop assistants as a reaction to their own Irish accent, often keenly felt by women and adolescents accustomed to the more relaxed manners of Ireland. All this, of course, is taken in stride by the average well–adjusted immigrant and the passage of time, of necessity, blunts such prickly first–impressions. But where these sensitivities can be critical is in the cases of immigrants already vulnerable through personality disorders. In this regard, the Irish authorities have little to be proud of, having condoned through successive generations the export of Ireland's mentally ill to Britain. The failures of the post–Revolutionary Irish Governments are legion, but in the context of this chapter, their neglect of the Irish émigrés is relevant.

In the past fifty years of independence, Irish Governments have paid only the minimum of attention to that other third of their population who resided semi–permanently in Britain. They did little to alleviate the travel conditions of the thirties, forties, and fifties when thousands of émigrés travelled to Britain in overcrowded, insanitary conditions reminiscent of the coffin–ships of the previous century.

They offered little active encouragement towards the setting up of welfare centres, though one of the recommendations of a Government–sponsored commission, *On Emigration and other Population Problems*,[21] had been that the Government should urgently provide such aid. Indeed the general feeling at Government level in the forties and fifties was one of gratitude that Britain provided a safety–valve for the excess of unemployed, or as one of the commission's members, Mr Alex Fitzgerald, said: 'High emigration . . . releases social tensions which would otherwise explode and makes possible a stability of manners and customs which would otherwise be subject to radical change.'

Mr Fitzgerald also declined to accept the view that 'a high rate of emigration is necessarily a sign of national decline. It is clear that in the history of the Catholic Church, the rôle of Irish emigrants has been significant. In the order of values, it seems more important to preserve and improve the quality of Irish life and therefore the purity of that message which our people have communicated to the world, than it is to reduce the numbers of Irish emigrants.' Those published remarks in 1953 were doubtless of immense consolation to the 33,000 emigrants who left Ireland that year and who were, for the most part, unwilling economic deportees. As they trudged off the mail-boats which daily berthed at Holyhead, their sense of abandonment must indeed have been lightened by the knowledge that their departure thus maintained 'the purity of that message which our people have communicated to the world'. They could, perhaps, have taken similar consolation from the views of one Irish historian of the period, who noted that 'had it not been for the safety-valve of emigration (400,000 in round figures for the decade 1950–60) the frustration of those years in Ireland would have led to mass riots.'

The immigrant boats, for the record, were depressing experiences—huddled anxious families, punctuated by the more ribald adolescents masking their uncertainty with hollow carousing. Then the bleary–eyed arrival into some strange city in the bleak hours and, for those without contacts, a trudge through strange streets in search of accommodation and eventually, work. Hardly surprising then that the inadequate and disturbed shortly found themselves in the care of one of the British welfare agencies.

What agencies in the peak–departure decade of the fifties attempted to help the inadequate? Not the Irish Government, as we have seen. Not the Irish middle–classes in Britain, fearful of their delicate (and imagined) status. The burden, in fact, lay with the British voluntary agencies who initiated sporadic measures, as did Irish Catholic lay organizations, such as the Legion of Mary and Knights of St Columba. In the event, the Catholic Hierarchy in Ireland made the first meaningful moves. Under pressure from priests in Britain the Irish Hierarchy established a scheme of emigrant chaplains who were assigned to areas of high Irish habitation. From the reports of these priests, telling of poor housing and high-drinking and the isolation of the single labourer, came the decision to establish welfare centres with resident chaplains. The centres got under way in the late fifties and their subsequent accelerated growth is a comment not only (and obviously) on the need for such places, but on the range of difficulties faced by immigrants in integrating, even functionally, into native British society.

A measure of these difficulties is the figure of over 5,000 interviews/services rendered by the centres in 1970, a year in which 30,000 Irish entered Britain. In London, the centre at Camden Square provided help of one sort or another to 1,741 persons; the major efforts being in the areas of accommodation (1,337 services) and employment (997 services). The centre also helped thirty–three unmarried mothers and 105 cases of mental disturbance (schizophrenia, paranoia, acute depression). Five hundred of those assisted returned during the year for after–care help.

In the fifteen years since founding, the London centre has dealt with increased custom in each successive year. Together with the Liverpool and Birmingham centres, it has borne the brunt of welfare demands and is currently being expanded to double its size, with the emphasis on additional hostel accommodation and services. In 1970, the Catholic Hierarchy in Ireland sponsored a 'once only' national collection for emigrants to Britain: of the £¼ million raised at church doors in Ireland, the bulk will be distributed among the centres in Britain to further what is, by any standard, a pioneering effort of ethnic self–help. Every area of major urban habitation now holds an Irish Centre, most of which are staffed with social workers. These centres are distinct from Irish clubs or dance–halls which have long been rooted in émigré areas and which mainly serve as drinking and dancing premises. The centres, by contrast, are engaged in energy and resource–stretching welfare work. Although they present a surfeit of things Irish, concerts, dancing-classes, bacon-and-cabbage dinners, underneath lies a concerned commitment to the upgrading of the emigrant's lot at the critical levels of housing, employment and general welfare.

Regionally, the brunt of such work is borne by the centres in London, Liverpool, Manchester, and Birmingham. Smaller conurbations tend naturally to have a smaller number of problem cases and in many cases the Irish immigrants in provincial towns seem, even proportionately, to present fewer problems. One reason is that chronic housing shortage and urban stress upon the personality are metropolitan phenomena. The other reason may be that the majority of rural–originating émigrés find themselves more at home in a provincial town than in a large city. In Bristol, Gloucester, and Portsmouth for instance, the Irish appear to blend more easily into the native fabric, to be more accepted as individuals and to form more valid relationships with the native population.

Cultural differences between England, Scotland, and Wales may be perceived in reaction to Irish immigration. Scotland is almost akin to Ulster in the separation of the communities in entrenched areas of Edinburgh and Glasgow: in that latter city, in the remnants of the Motherwell and Gorbals ghettos, the inherited seige–mentality persists. Football encounters between Rangers and Celtic teams are occasions for ritualistic displays of tribal extremism with Rangers being urged on to prove Scots-Protestant supremacy over the Celtic Irish–Catholic representation. All local police leave is cancelled for the year's series of matches and on the day following such encounters local magistrates are faced with an inevitable list of defendants. Rangers field non-Catholic players; Celtic mainly Catholic ones;

Celtic fly the Irish tricolour, and travel abroad on Aer Lingus planes. The ghostly figures of the Protestant King William of Orange and the Catholic King James stalk the consciousness of the working districts of Glasgow, demanding due tribal loyalty from each successive generation of immigrants, a loyalty which, if emotively rendered, encourages the donor to risk appearing as a statistic in the city's annual crime figures. Given the sectarian traditions of Glasgow, it is hardly surprising to note that a higher proportion of Protestant Irish emigrants from Ulster arrive there annually than to any other single conurbation in Britain.

In the rural areas of Scotland, Irish immigration follows the pattern laid down in the previous century's tradition of seasonal harvesting, potato–picking, and farm labouring, a tradition encased in the emigrant culture of the counties of Mayo and Donegal on the north-western Irish seaboard. Until the 1950s, whole families from these counties seasonally migrated to gather in the harvest in Ayrshire, Stirlingshire, Fife, and the Lothians, where each large farm had its 'bothie', a sort of open shed, which housed the migrant harvesters. They were paid according to their rate of clearance, at so much an acre harvested, and though they slept on straw beds and other facilities were primitive, in warm weather the system generally worked well.

By the fifties, however, a sinister element evolved. Whereas formerly local farmers contracted their own particular group of harvesters from Ireland, and generally treated them well, by the late fifties, a sort of Irish 'middle-man' had developed, intent on procuring maximum profit by offering their own working gangs to farmers. At this time the family migratory tradition had diminished, to be replaced with a flotsam of the inadequate and the delinquent. The outcome was the growth of an 'Irish Mafia' of contractors who brutalized their charges into excessive hours at low wages, and maintained, literally, a reign of terror over sections of the migrant labour. Workers who objected to the low wages were physically beaten, school–age youngsters were prevented from returning to Ireland, young girls were inveigled into promiscuity. It was, for the record, exploitation by the Irish upon the Irish.

Following newspaper revelations in the summer of 1971, the

Scottish authorities attempted to alleviate the more blatant cases of hardship, but it is doubtful if the iniquities have been more than temporarily contained.

In Wales, few such sub–civilized ghettos exist. Indeed, of the three countries which make up Britain, Wales appears to offer the most relaxed and encouraging process of absorption. The 'continuum' of previous generations' descendants are representative of all levels of Welsh society and offer a hospitable texture of acceptance, extending in some instances to areas of employment which favour not only Welsh–Irish but present-day Irish immigrants. The work–force of a particular Cardiff factory, for instance, has since the 1900s been almost exclusively Irish, a protective reaction, perhaps, to the thunderings of Baptist preachers at the invading Catholic–Irish 'hordes' of the late nineteenth century. With growing urbanization the formerly strong religious identity of the Welsh has diminished somewhat and with it the strong antagonism towards the Irish has become diluted. And with the revival of Welsh self–assertion and nationalism, the immigrant Irish are becoming more accepted as allies rather than intruders.

In discussing the Irish émigrés as a 'social problem', due cognizance must be taken of the element of socio–cultural hostility which a minority still encounter in diverse areas. Anti-social behaviour in any immigrant group must to some degree be a response to native hostility. A possible pointer to the level of hostility, nationwide, was provided in a Gallup Survey of October 1967 which asked the question:

Do you think that on the whole this country has benefited or been harmed through immigrants coming to settle here from Ireland?

Answer:

Benefited 16 per cent; *Harmed* 22 per cent; No difference 46 per cent; Don't know 16 per cent.

In the cities of England, by and large, there is little overt antagonism and the work of the Irish centres can concentrate on those issues of housing and employment which are critical to anyone's sense of well–being, immigrant or no. In the welfare office of the Irish Centre in London's Camden Square, for

instance, new immigrants and others requiring help are pro-
cessed professionally: an extensive file of contacts is daily
tapped for aid with employment and accommodation, the latter
being chronically important and in chronically short supply to
the immigrant inflow into the burgeoning capital.

Such has been the overall contribution of such services—
and of the chaplains and social workers—that the weight of
Irish 'social problems' upon native British agencies has decreased
in the last decade.[22] By contrast, some of the techniques evolved
from dealing with the problems of the Irish have been success-
fully applied to the wider British community at large.

The progress of one emigrant chaplain, Father Eamonn
Casey, provides a dramatic example of such feedback.
Casey, a tough-minded fluent priest from County Limerick,
arrived as chaplain to the Irish community in Slough in
1960. His arrival coincided with the expansion of the town,
with the growth of industry there and with the attendant
increase in the numbers of Irish families and workers.
In his view much of the disorientation, insecurity, and
high alcoholic consumption he encountered among the Irish
had one salient cause – shortage of decent, economically-priced
housing. From that shortage, Father Casey felt, flowed most of
the other symptoms of anti-social behaviour, particularly as the
housing shortage most critically affected Irish families, most of
whom, with families larger than the British average,[23] found it
impossible to achieve home–ownership. Father Casey's solution
was two–pronged. First, to raise a 'bank' of capital from the
well-off, and secondly to raise the savings ability of those in
need. With priestly persistence he succeeded in both. Local
industrialists and a sympathetic minority of local middle–classes
were tapped for funds; with this initial 'bank' property was
acquired and renovated and needful families installed at
economic rents: for those who could afford more realistic rents,
a proportion was held by Father Casey towards eventual house
purchase on mortgage. A year after beginning there was
sufficient inflow of capital in rents and savings and gifts to
institute a system of financial gearing which maximized available
(and growing) funds. From the priest's efforts and urging
towards self–help grew a housing society which became expert

F

in exploiting the hitherto disparate resources of local authority, family budgets, socialist–minded professional people and building societies; to produce, within the capitalistic framework, a system socialist in attitude. The pioneering Slough effort made deep inroads upon the housing problems as well as other social problems, of the local Irish community. It also occurred at a time of nationwide housing problems; the blueprint has subsequently been adapted by other local authorities, particularly those with substantial immigrant communities, such as the London boroughs of Camden and Lambeth.

In other cities, the Catholic Housing Aid Society had been working along similar lines and in 1963 Father Casey became National Director of that body. Blooded, so to speak, by the Slough success, Casey now applied his expertise, and that of his lieutenants, to the wider national field. As National Director of the Society, Casey housed seven thousand people in the following five years of his directorship. Each successive year saw the Society move out from a Catholic–Irish base, into the wider community at large. Whereas in the early years the Irish accounted for 60 per cent of clients, the proportion of Irish has now levelled out at a third and the Catholic Housing Aid Society has become an influential agency of help to the community generally.[24]

Thus in the past decade the social and settlement problems among the Irish have been tackled in the main by the Irish themselves. Most of the credit is due to the Irish Hierarchy, a body which rarely finds itself the object of praise from social scientists. (It could be argued that the traditional policies of the Catholic Church, in areas of education and family planning, are partially responsible for problems among emigrants.) Nevertheless, at a time when a potent minority among the Irish in Britain desperately needed help, when the British welfare agencies did their statutory best, the only other source from which intimate, professional help was forthcoming was from the Irish Catholic Hierarchy.

Growing numbers of young priests were assigned to Britain in the fifties and sixties, many of them with new training in the social sciences. For a high proportion, the experience was salutary and disconcerting. They were, for the most part, pro-

ducts of Catholic families whose acceptance of the Church's
teachings was total. Suddenly they encountered among the
emigrant Irish attitudes which threatened their acceptance of
unquestioned doctrine. More severely were the unconscious
assumptions of Irish society thrown into sharp isolation;
assumptions about the behaviour of adolescents, about the
mobility of the men, and the chastity of the women. Working
in the twilight areas of large cities, they encountered the Irishmen with common-law wives, Irishwomen engaged in
prostitution, and adolescent drug–addicts. For a few the conflict between the mythology fondly fostered by the home society
(all Irishmen are pure, the women chaste, the adolescents innocent), and the reality of daily case–work was overwhelming
and resulted in breakdown. During one year in the sixties, I
understand, half a dozen of the fifty priests involved were
repatriated because of ill–health. The point was taken by the
Hierarchy. Now potential emigrant chaplains spend work
periods in Britain during their training.

Certainly for the orthodox–minded priest, some of the personal ailments met with in a seething city could be bewildering.
One priest in a North London parish assured me that what
most of his callers needed was not a priest but a psychiatrist
and he regarded his previous years in Africa as soft compared
with the demands upon him in his London parish. His com-
ments may be more relevant than he thought: many of his
Irish callers were brought up in a society where the priest
occupied a position which incorporated elements of the witch-
doctor and the psychiatrist. But whether the traditional priestly
training in Ireland is sufficient to cope with the complicated
ills endemic in high-stress urban living is another matter.

To put it simply, the recitation of the Sixth Command-
ment to a young unmarried mother is obviously of less
use than some basic instruction in elementary techniques
of family planning. But hardly any priests are equipped
to render such advice (even if allowed to do so) and most
lay social workers at Irish centres are loth to prescribe any
advice at variance with Church teaching. Similarly, applicants
with maritial problems which are rooted in conflict over methods of contraception cannot be offered objective medical help.

Thus, in some elementary areas of Irish social work, the very system most involved is severely hampered by its own religious attitudes. Some chaplains and social workers privately admit this, and even criticize the narrow spectrum of Irish education generally. But until some further enlightenment affects the powers–that–be, there is little these workers in the field can do. At the time of writing there is little prospect of such advance, for almost all Irish education is controlled by the Church and though the creation of twenty–five Community Schools initially offered hope for a liberal-humanist education, that prospect too has dimmed. Speaking in Dublin in October 1971, the Primate of Ireland, Dr McQuaid, declared that the proposed Community Schools would be: 'Catholic in their management and teaching staff, in their discipline and curriculum...' During the following month, opening a medical centre in the same city, the Archbishop implied that the centre —which trains one in three of the Republic's doctors in gynaecology—would not provide tuition in the general medical aspects of contraception. It wasn't until 1969 that Biology was introduced as a schools subject in Ireland, and then on a meagre level. Until recently there was no sex–education for the Republic's school-children (two out of five of whom on present trends will emigrate) which may account, in part, for the fact that Irish–born patients accounted for three-quarters of all European immigrants attending British clinics for the treatment of venereal diseases in 1962.[25]

Similarly, many factors which combine to produce inadequate emigrants can be traced to the Irish educational system, in particular to the dominating influence of the Church. It is, of course, merely a truism to recite that many of the characteristics in any society which make for inadequate adults can be traced to that society's socio–educational system, but it is a truism which, on evidence, cannot be too often emphasized.

Certainly any concerned study of the problems among a substantial minority of the Irish in Britain must inevitably lead to a penetrating evaluation of the educational structure in Ireland. On present attitudes, any such radical evaluation is unlikely to be countenanced, although confidential reports from the emigrant chaplains must provide stimulus for hard–thinking among the Catholic Hierarchy. One such report, currently with the Hierarchy, was compiled from an experimental case–work study among Irish immigrant adolescents in London during 1969–71.

The case–work was conducted at Benburb Base in the borough of Camden—which gave generous help to the experiment—and around five hundred Irish adolescents were offered help in coming to terms with a wide variety of problems ranging from the relatively simple matters of jobs and accommodation to the more taxing demands of personality disorders. There were, too, cases of naïve prostitution among young girls, and cases of petty criminality among male teenagers. The most common symptom, in the social workers' judgements, was a feeling of loneliness which they felt was traceable to early family conflicts in Ireland, a loneliness which the victims hoped would ease with the transference across the Irish Sea, only to find that the new pressures of urban living in a strange environment compounded these problems. Benburb Base, under the care of a Belfast priest with training and experience in social work (and therefore no stranger to such contemporary urban–stress problems) has enjoyed some success in its experimental first year's effort.[26] The report of its findings and recommendations, currently before the Irish Hierarchy—and the body's reaction—will determine the future character and scope of the Base's efforts.

Thus in another critical area of immigrant vulnerability during the last decade have the Irish made inroads upon their 'social problems'. There are signs that the momentum of such self–help will gather pace, from the combination of increased awareness among the Irish community generally and the greater interest evinced among young social workers in Ireland. One area of distress, however, has been neglected – the area of drink and alcoholism.

ALCOHOL AND ALCOHOLISM

In 1966, when Irish–born formed 3 per cent of the population of London, a study of London's 'Skid Row' showed that the Irish formed 37 per cent of the sample studied. (Tabulated from the *Lancet* 29 January 1966.) And the report of the

Council for Social Welfare, 1970, was that Catholics in Britain have a higher proportion of alcoholics than any other religious denomination.

In the light of the above, it is almost facile to suggest that any discussion of alcoholism and the Irish should proceed from the acknowledgement that alcoholic drink permeates all levels of Irish life. Yet it is a necessary premise from which to proceed, for it explains the failure to contain the problem, and the reluctance to tackle a ruinous disease. The fact is that alcohol is enshrined in Irish life, and has been for centuries. In rhyme and rann, song and story, drink has become something of a sanctified Irish institution, by turns cursed and praised but never, in active consumption, ignored:

> Be you Cook's son, Earl's son or Duke's son
> Not one penny goes past the tombstone's brink
> So join the chorus, we've life before us
> When we put our one true trust in drink
>   – from the Gaelic of 'Preab san Ol'
>   (Trust in Drink) by Brendan Behan

It is tempting, as in so many other areas of Irish life, for Irishmen to simply blame the English for the national weakness for alcohol. History is rife with such comforting evidence and the case is easy to construct. One could begin with the fact that alcoholic drink is a reliever of stress and of untenable situations, and proceed to demonstrate that the vicissitudes of Anglo–Irish history reduced the Irish psyche to a state of stress lasting for centuries. Studies among Red Indians in America, for example, showed drinking habits (and underlying psychological attitudes) not dissimilar to the besieged state of the Irish peasantry in recent centuries.

One could show that the essential psychological attractions of drink, the sense of escapism and hazy well-being, are particularly relevant to a people born and living with a sense of inherited dispossession. One could thus so easily place the burden of moral culpability elsewhere and yet be left with the problem and the overriding evidence that from within the Irish community little effort has been made to contain it. Indeed,

membership of the Irish community is to be statistically more
prone to becoming part of the problem. As a London conference on Alcoholism was told in 1970: 'In Alcoholics
Anonymous they say you don't have to be Irish or Catholic
but it gives you a headstart.' The speaker, an Irish social
worker (and former alcoholic) declared that 25 per cent of the
treatment beds maintained by the Salvation Army in London
were occupied by Irish vagrants, yet the total number of such
beds attributable to Irish–Catholic agencies was minute: $2\frac{1}{2}$
per cent or in the region of 55 beds as against the Salvation
Army's 2,100 in London alone.[27] In other areas of rehabilitation and after–care concern for alcoholics, the proportion of
Irish candidates is similarly high, while the Irish share of
help is dramatically low. Undoubtedly the disparity is due to
the peculiar position of drink in the Irish ethos, and the attendant intricate attitudes towards those who become addicted.
Generally, there is a marked reluctance to face the reality of
addiction: the word 'alcoholic' being regarded as an impolite
noun in many levels of Irish society. Rather there exists a
gamut of euphemisms which cushion the medical reality.
Phrases such as: 'He has a liking for the hard stuff' are used
to describe what is most often a condition of whisky addiction.
Or, 'he has a weakness for the drop' may sentimentally cloak
the distress of a friend or colleague who cannot see the day
through without a substantial intake of alcohol. Indeed addiction sometimes takes on the aura of praise: 'The good man's
fault', a commonplace expression, reflects the inherited sexual
puritanism of the lower middle classes: the implication being
that indulgence in drink is less culpable than indulgence in sex.

I do not suggest that a heady devotion to Bacchus is the
sole prerogative of the Irish—the Scots, French, and Russians
have a similar devotion—but rather attempt to express the
underlying resistance faced by those involved in rehabilitating
the substantial number of Irish alcoholics. That such rescue
efforts have met with success is a matter of recorded fact
among the many agencies, particularly in London, who deal
with alcoholics.[28]

I am grateful to one such agency, the Camberwell Council
on Alcoholism, for permission to publish the following case

history of rehabilitation of one Irish victim. It does, I think, illustrate not only what is possible in terms of cure, but illuminates also many of the factors which are at the root of 'social problems' among the immigrant Irish.

'IT NEVER SEEMED A PROBLEM TO ME'
An interview with an Irish alcoholic

When did you start drinking?

Regularly from about sixteen.

When did it become a problem to you?

I know now when drink became a problem to me. Years ago I would never go to pubs before first coming home and washing and dressing after work. I would go to the lounge bars on Saturdays and Sundays and meet girls, and think it was a wonderful social life. The downfall started when I began going about with the Irish lads, and working in the building trade, getting £3 a day instead of a regular job. We'd get back from work at six or seven at night, and go into pubs in our working clothes, then the importance of keeping myself tidy seemed to slip away without me knowing it. People began ignoring me, so I stopped going to those pubs. I started going into lower-type pubs, sliding into the East End part of town where every one was in their working clothes, and where people didn't notice me and accepted me that way. I never noticed myself much either, but the digs kept getting poorer and slummier and the old landladies harder.

I never felt it because I thought I was enjoying myself, and I was that sick the next morning that I couldn't care less where I was. On the days I was sober, I was just working for drink. Then I stopped eating, started saying that a cheese sandwich and a cup of tea is the price of a few pints. I notice these things now, but I never noticed them then. As long as I was getting drink I didn't care.

Eventually I got to the stage where I couldn't keep digs, so I went to Rowton Houses and 'Sallies', but I got barred from them, so I began sleeping out. This was about five years ago.

The routine in the last three drinking years in London was to go to the Fish Market at five in the morning and do odd casual jobs, going in and out of the pub till two in the afternoon. Then I'd get two bottles of wine, a bottle of 'jack' and a bottle of cider. When I'd drunk that I'd be drunk the rest of the day. It put me in a sort of delirium, a couldn't-care-less sort of attitude; it didn't make me drunk – it knocked me stupid. I was walking about in a sort of mist.

How frequently have you been arrested for being drunk?

Two or three times a week since I was eighteen.

Did the police ever ask you about your drinking?

Many a time when they took my particulars they'd say, 'This drink's going to kill you. Are you not going to do something about it?'

Have you ever been to prison?

Yes.

Was drinking always the cause?

Every time I was in gaol drink was always in me when I got caught. I've never done anything criminal in cold-blooded sobriety in my life.

When you were arrested did anyone ever offer you help?

I was never approached, even in prison, no.

From what you know now, when was the first time someone should have said, 'You have a problem. You need help'?

From what I know of alcoholism now, I think if I had got the same chances ten years ago as I got two years ago, I might have been able to do something with them. But was it up to anyone to approach me? I don't know; perhaps I should have had more sense.

What was happening to you ten years ago?

I was living in Birmingham in a single room in the same house with my married brother and sister, and working regularly in

F*

the building trade. At that time I would drink from Thursday to Sunday. The rest of the week would be sort of hell, but I always seemed to manage some way.

Did you contact anyone at that time who could have helped you?

I never went officially to see anyone, but I had to go to hospital after I fell off a roof while I was at work.

Were you drunk when you fell?

No, but I was very drunk the night before, so you may guess it was through the effects of drink. I was rushed into casualty with a broken leg and arm and six broken ribs.

Did they go into why you fell off the roof?

No. They asked me what happened and where I lived. It seemed to me that they were not too keen on letting me stay in hospital.

Why not?

I don't know ... I've never thought about it. I suppose because I was an Irishman and they smelt the fumes of drink off me.

Do you think they could have realized that you had a drinking problem?

I think today they would. There's more being done for alcoholics and more talk about it. But you see, I never had a problem as far as I was concerned. I was living my allotted life, I just accepted it.

When were you first offered help?

Five years ago. A policeman asked me if I was an alcoholic when he found me in a 'skipper' in Bristol. He told me that it was a pity that I had got myself into such a state, as I was only a young man. I said, 'What do you mean? I'm no alcoholic.'

Did he explain what he meant by an alcoholic?

No, but he said there were people you could go to for help. I didn't know what he was talking about, and I wasn't interested at three o'clock in the morning. He gave me a doctor's card and told me to get myself cleaned up when I got paid on Thursday and go down and see the doctor. I didn't do anything about it. I thought an alcoholic was someone who had to drink a bottle of whisky a day. I hadn't heard much talk of them, but when I'd seen them in films they were always rich people.

And you didn't associate them with yourself?

No, you see, everyone I knew was in the same condition as myself and I thought it was the natural thing; I just accepted it.

What happened after the policeman spoke to you?

I was very ill so went and stayed at a 'spike' just outside the city from Christmas to March. My nerves were in a terrible state. I never had a drink all that time, though I went to work every day. I was too ill to be bothered with the drink.

Had you made a decision not to drink?

No. I had no intentions of giving up the drink, but it was a very cold winter, and the 'spike' was out in the country. If I'd had any drink in me at all they would have thrown me out. I had got used to the bed, and didn't want to give it up. It was the first time maybe, now that I think about it, that I realized that I had to stay sober for some reason.

Why did you leave?

The money had piled up at the Labour Exchange so I took it and came to London, and then I spent three years knocking about the East End. That was when I first began to get the D.T.s and the shakes really badly.

Did you ever go to hospital?

I was in the casualty department six or seven times, after being hit on the head with bottles and things. They would patch me up and throw me out.

Did they ever do anything more?

Nothing at all. I never saw a social worker or anyone of that kind.

Where did you finally get help?

When I was in the Reception Centre one time, one of the staff asked me to stop in seven days because I was in such a state. Then I saw a doctor there.

How did he help you?

He was marvellous. He deliberately went out of his way to make me angry. I now realize that it was the treatment exactly I needed at the time. We used to nearly come to blows, but at night I couldn't go to sleep for thinking about what he had told me. I didn't always agree with him, but at least he started making me use my mind about myself. Whether I agreed with him or not wasn't the point.

Had you accepted that you were an alcoholic?

Not at first. I was sober in the Centre six weeks and then I went and got drunk for a month before coming back for three months.

Why didn't you go on drinking?

I couldn't. I was feeling really physically ill, worse than when I went in the first time.

Why did you go back to the Centre?

Because of the feeling of conscience I had. It was the first time it really hit me I was throwing away an opportunity. I was drinking with a guilty conscience and feeling that I was deliberately doing something wrong. I wasn't getting any pleasure out of drinking, and for the first time I worried about my condition the next morning. I began realizing that the people at the Centre weren't talking rubbish, and that maybe I *was* an alcoholic. This member of staff at the Centre had really gone out of his way to talk to me; he was the first person who ever took a personal interest in me at all, not only about the drinking, but about everything. He explained a lot about life concerning myself, and I knew he was talking sense. So I went back. The minute he saw me he said he had expected me and that he knew I had something in me, and that I'd come back.

Where did you go from the Centre?

I was on the waiting list to go to a hostel. The doctor called me in one day and said that there was a good hostel nearby and asked me to go to see a psychiatrist about getting in there. The idea of a psychiatrist frightened me; one time when I was in a Centre in the country the warden threatened that he would have me certified by a psychiatrist. But I went to the hospital to see this one about the hostel and I liked him from the moment I saw him. He was very quiet and didn't ask me many questions. Then he asked me if I would be willing to let him try to help me. I agreed, and went into the hostel the following week.

How did you get on in the hostel?

The Group Therapy meetings kept me on my mettle. I was a rebel right from the beginning, but if you go into these hostels to be a model pupil, they can't help you. You've got to be honest with yourself and sincere, and not worry about sounding nice and agreeable at the meetings. I was also helped whilst I was there by friends I made outside; they weren't alcoholics. I met them through going to help voluntarily the different organizations that give aid to drinking alcoholics and homeless men in general. They gave me a lot of encouragement and personal interest and would explain and help me with things that came up at meetings.

How long have you been sober now?

Two years.

And why do you remain sober?

When I was drinking, before I went to the Reception Centre, I was in complete ignorance. I lost everything by degrees and I never missed it going. I never sat down and looked at what I missed through drinking. It never seemed a problem to me. I couldn't slip into that state again – I've learnt so much in the last two years. I couldn't unconsciously throw away my life the way I did before. There would be no innocence behind it if I drank again.

There are many clues in that interview which highlight factors relevant to the entire ethos of Irish immigration. It may be noted that the subject began to go downhill when he became 'involved with the Irish lads and working in the building trade'.

The observation occurs that he found some more fulfilling measure of identity there, among those who, bereft of other social alternatives, make the pub their social centre of warmth and cameraderie.

'It seemed to me they were not too keen on letting me stay in hospital . . . because I was an Irishman and they smelt the fumes of drink'. A classic example of the sense of alienation felt by many immigrants, an alienation most comfortably cloaked in spurious comradeship of the pub. Further, the subject registered the feeling, exaggerated most often among groups of Irish building workers, of unspoken hostility on the dual grounds of dress and nationality. 'I was in the casualty department six or seven times, after being hit on the head . . . they would patch me up and throw me out.'

'Just another drunken Paddie' may well have been the reaction of an overworked hospital staff. Someone else, however, had a more humane view: '[the doctor] was marvellous... We used to nearly come to blows but at night I couldn't go to sleep for thinking about what he had told me . . . *he was the first person who ever took an interest in me at all* . . . He explained a lot about life concerning myself, and I knew he was talking sense.'

There are, one feels, many pointers in that interview which may account for the excessive numbers of Irish in Britain who form that sub–group of afflicted flotsam. It is a telling commentary upon the self–lauded claims of 'Christian Ireland' that every year a proportion of her emigrants to Britain will—by that first step aboard the emigrant boat—also head for the loneliness and humiliation of the alcoholically afflicted. Whatever the personality factors during their time in Ireland which predispose them to becoming addicts in Britain, the fact is that concerned, professional help from among the Irish community in Britain is almost non-existent; an area of neglect in stark contrast to some other achievements of self-help. Given that record of self-help, particularly during the past decade, it may be reasonable to assume that in time similar inroads will be made upon this area of human need. At the time of writing, however, such confidence is based more on optimism than on fact.

9

The Settled Community

The 'community' feeling among the million Irish–born who reside, for the most part, permanently in Britain is a comparatively recent development and certainly within the confines of the last decade. They had, hitherto, been regarded as a community more by their hosts than by themselves, and even now tended to be regarded, as former Labour Government Minister Roy Hattersley wrote in *The Times* in February 1971, '... as all the same. To their detractors they appear uniformly violent and unskilled, with a pick–axe in one hand, a bottle of stout in the other and the name of a building contractor stencilled on their backs. Even their champions often mount no more persuasive a defence than our duty to be grateful for the railways, canals and roads that could not have been built without them. Ireland's disproportionately large contribution to the British Army's General Staff is usually overlooked.'

It is not, of course, only to the General Staff of the British Army that the present Irish presence is to be noted, but more characteristically among the 10,000 Irish–born who form around 6 per cent of the 172,000-strong land forces. And though the shape and walk of the Irish navvies still predominate on the building sites, the 'name of a building contractor stencilled upon their backs' is increasingly likely to be an Irish one. And while popular reaction may see as typically Irish the boozy antics of a drunk on a late–night train, the policeman who books the drunk into a cell for the night might well be as Irish. Residual images, however, persist. As reported in an issue of the Birmingham *Evening Mail* of November 1965, the then Lord Mayor, Mr Corbyn–Barrow, noted: 'If you look at the list of persons for trial at the Quarter Sessions, you will realize what difficulties there are in assimilating the Irish into the life of the city. As you look down the list, you will see it is almost entirely Irish names.'

His remarks, by no means unusual at the time, reflected an image of the Irish which, however validly based, sounded echoes of unease among the growing segment of middle–class and 'voluntary' immigrants of recent years, and among those of previous generations who in the sixties had evolved to a sense of fruitful adjustment to their lives in Britain. From mixed motives of self–interest—'to upgrade the image' and social responsibility—'let's help our less fortunate'—there evolved some sense of community awareness, characterized by the activities of the Federation of Irish Societies. Founded in Portsmouth in 1964 by, perhaps predictably, three Corkmen (of professional occupation), the Federation subsequently pro– vided the embryo structure wherein the various, and previously disparate, Irish organizations may cohesively contribute towards community self–help, notably in the expansion of Irish centres and the attendant growth of welfare facilities. In this regard, the Federation was instrumental in securing substantial finan– cial loans for the Bass Charrington Brewery towards the pur– chase of premises for centres and in 1972 the Federation spon– sored a conference of delegates from forty Irish societies to formulate a cohesive approach to welfare and 'social problems', an indication of the growing sense of independence, and reality, towards the permanence of the Irish community in Britain.

This sense of permanence, however, raises questions of identity and attitude. How Irish are the Irish in Britain?

It is a question not easily answered, for the only immediate comparison can be with the Irish in Ireland who themselves reflect many diverse traits, and in some respects a minority of the settled Irish in Britain appear more Irish than the Irish in Ireland. At many Irish clubs, for instance, the playing of the Irish National Anthem is attended with more respect than at any similar gathering in Ireland (except in the Catholic areas of Ulster). Similarly the surfeit of shamrocks, tricolours, and patriot portraits which adorn most Irish clubs in Britain would appear incongruous and dated in establishments in the Republic. Likewise, the degree of enthusiasm displayed by parents in having their children avail of Irish dancing classes, for which there is an extensive waiting list, appears almost excessive to casual visitors from Ireland. For such supporters of things Irish in Britain there is little self–doubt as to their sense of identity, although it may appear to the outside observer that such devotion to cultural insignia reflects an unwillingness to adjust to the more cosmopolitan possibilities of their new environment.

Certainly the gamut of institutional symbols is wide–ranging, from regular attendance at Sunday Mass and the weekly purchase of newspapers from Ireland, to the unfailing trip home every year, all of which serve as reassurance of identity and which may superficially appear to offer evidence of unsettlement in Britain, but which on reflection may be more accurately judged as the compensatory needs of those who have, in fact, settled. Accordingly, some contact with things Irish serves as a reminder of another country, to which the other Irish for the most part are unlikely to return to permanent habitation. For in spite of their green–tinted praise of the virtues of Ireland, immigrants display a marked reluctance to return home in any meaningful numbers. 'The Banks of My Own Lovely Lee', as Dominic Behan has remarked, are especially lovely to Corkmen on a Saturday night in Kilburn— happily two hundred miles away from the self–same banks.

They remain, nevertheless, Irish in many aspects of temperament; in their (for the most part) adherence to Catholicism, in their suspicion of 'pagan' values, and in their hard-headed awareness of economic reality. When the *Irish Post* asked of its readers: 'Given an equivalent income, would you return to live permanently in Ireland?' 85 per cent answered yes, yet nowhere near that proportion have in fact returned in recent years, in spite of the greatly improved economic situation in the sixties which would have provided many returned emigrants with an equivalent income in real terms.

Why then have not more returned? The answer is almost totally economic, involving many complicated factors. A random questioning conducted by this writer among Irish-born showed that while the most widespread single response was a straight economic one: 'better pay and living conditions', other economically-influenced factors were almost as weighty, including a distrust of the Irish economy and, among the middle-aged, a residual memory of 'hard times' in Ireland. In the case of parents, a potent reason was a marked reluctance to uproot their children from what they regarded as better educational opportunities and future career prospects in Britain.

Outside of economic considerations, some respondents simply felt that they were happier in Britain than in Ireland, and enjoyed the stimulation of cosmopolitan life, in particular the forging of friendships with non–Irish people, while the longer-settled displayed some unease at the real or imagined problems of re–settling in Ireland. More than half, however, said they would return to Ireland 'sometime', an answer which betrays some measure of self–deception; as mentioned earlier, available figures indicate a much lesser number returning to permanent habitation in recent years. Nevertheless, almost all regarded themselves as Irish and could not foresee themselves formally adopting British nationality, while a minority displayed signs of trenchant Irishness in the sense of frequenting Irish clubs, regularly reading the *Irish Post* and reacting strongly to what they see as evidence of stock English attitudes towards them.

Observer journalist Patrick O'Donovan has written of 'the predictable flood of letters to the editor whenever anything remotely controversial is written about religion or Ireland. These are formidable letters and the most daunting come from Irish Catholics who live in England and who, like pain-maddened buffaloes, attack on sight. And they savage you, not only for what you said, but for not saying what they think you ought to have said. I sometimes feel that this particular sort of exile is activated by unconscious guilt about not being in Ireland.'

Whatever the likely truth of that last assertion—and it may indeed explain the excessive Irishness of a minority—the prickly sensitivity can be potent, as the *Irish Post* painfully discovered. Some months after the paper was launched (with a green–inked masthead and the slogan: 'The Voice of the Irish in Britain') it published a front-page story headed 'Sex Goes Underground' which recited, half tongue-in-cheek, the plans of a well–known London–Irish publican and publicist, Buttie Sugrue, to bury underground a man and wife until such time as the wife conceived. Reaction from outraged members of the community was swift; the paper was promptly banned from sale outside many North London Catholic churches and the flow of abusive letters and telephone calls continued for some weeks. It was a curious phenomenon of sensitivity provoked more by the impression possibly given to non–Irish readers, rather than to any integral bad taste of the story itself, a classic reaction of 'what will the neighbours say?' (neighbours in this case being the British at large) and one which betokened a sense of insecure settlement. One indignant woman reader charged that 'it's the sort of story one expects to find in *The People* newspaper . . .' and when taxed she admitted that *The People* was read regularly in her home, but that 'we expect better from an Irish paper, especially a paper about the Irish in England.' It is the most obviously 'Irish' (including some with English accents) of the immigrants who generally display the strongest reaction to real or imagined slurs and who can hardly be strictly divided among class terms, but reflects rather the personal sense of security or adjustment of individuals. Predictably, the longer–settled tend to ignore, or even no longer notice, what the newcomer may be highly sensitive to; the Irish, after all, have been prominent as the butt of humour in the British consciousness for at least the past century, and it is entirely reasonable that most native–born British, when confronted with an Irish situation, should react from that inherited imagery of the Irish.

It may be relevant, nonetheless, to note the extent to which these automatic attitudes towards the Irish still persist. When thirty hours of video tape of the highly successful 1971 television series, 'The Comedians', was analysed it was found that: 'the jokes the comedians told in order of frequency were: 1. Anti–Pakistani, 2. Anti–Irish, 3. Anti–Semetic, 4. Anti–docker, 5. Sexual'.[29] On television the Irish drunk, villain or priest is almost a routine encounter in any one week's viewing, but a more revealing insight into unconscious attitudes was provided by writer Christopher Logue (admittedly Jesuit–educated and of Irish descent) when he translated a play of the Belgian writer

Hugo Claus for production at London's Royal Court Theatre in November 1971. *The Times* reviewer, having outlined the play which has incest as one of its themes, noted that 'it is hard ... to know how to divide credit between the Belgian author and his translator, Christopher Logue ... when the truth comes out about George's incest, what would be the Belgian equivalent of the reaction: "It's common enough among the Irish; but as for you, George, a rate-payer ... "?'

Undoubtedly the native attitudes expressed by the media affect the sense of Irishness among the immigrants, producing among the devotees a trenchant reinforcement of their nationality and perhaps contributing among the greater diffused proportion a conscious diluting of such obvious Irish characteristics as accent and turn of phrase. For it is among the greater proportion who do not frequent Irish clubs or surround themselves with the props of spurious identity that the true conflicts of identity occur; among those who have found their emigration rewarding, succeeding at their work and having valued friendships among the English; those who, in Conor Cruise O'Brien's phrase 'most experience their duality', that the pressures to transfer cultural and political loyalties are most severe. Said Roy Hattersley: '... the Irish are only totally accepted in British society when they lose their Irish characteristics. If their accent is obvious and if their children—being Catholic—do not attend the local school, there is the underlying suspicion that sooner or later they will come home blind drunk. The assumption is nonsense. But it is nevertheless dangerous, particularly so for Irishmen who want a mortgage, promotion or public office.'

The assumption was felt by the increasing number of middle–class Irish in the sixties who came in pursuit of mortgage and promotion—if not public office—and provided momentum for many to divest themselves, in so far as they could, of Irish extremities of accent or behaviour, leading, in some cases, to comical hybrids whose broad vowel sounds keep breaking through adopted genteel tones.

Such hybrids are, however, tiny in number; most of the 'middle–class' Irish in Britain are almost indistinguishable from their counterparts in Ireland, except perhaps in areas where, in this writer's experience, they tend to be more liberal in attitudes of sexual morality and less hidebound by anti–British feeling than the same class in Ireland. They are also, given the competitive nature of British metropolitan life, more industrious, have fewer children, and may be marginally wealthier; and, if the desire was sufficiently strong, could make the transfer back to Ireland with greater ease than, say, the mass of working–class Irish labour.

Accordingly, they may in many respects not feel the need to assert their Irishness here, preferring gently to absorb, and be absorbed into, the rituals of middle–class and upper middle–class English life which many find agreeable and stimulating. There is much written about the 'charm of the Irish', a much more potent force may be the 'charm of the English' and particularly the lure of certain English rituals of life–style which project an almost irresistible aura for many post-imperial Irish. It is no accident that the B.B.C. receives an inordinately large number of applications from Irishmen; that the various branches of the former Colonial Service were heavily staffed with Irish; that the Limerick–born actor Richard Harris was regarded as having brought off some sort of coup in marrying a Lord's daughter; or that the Right–Wing Monday Club, sometimes referred to as 'the conscience of Conservatives', contains some Irish–born members.

Even for the Irish in Ireland, influences arising from the proximity of Britain are widespread; tastes in clothes, reading matter and general life-style invariably follow—often after a ten–year interval—those of Britain, so that most emigrants to the larger island are already conditioned in many respects for absorption in their social stream in Britain. It is an absorption which, given the settlement of the Ulster issue, is likely to apply to the majority of immigrants, particularly when accompanied by material success and the forging of satisfactory careers. One successful architect, the beneficiary of such advances, gave his attitude as: 'being very reluctant to return to Ireland. Apart from the risk of lowering my standard of living, in other areas my life is better here; I have more trustworthy friends, and though it gives me no particular pleasure

to say so, I regard their attitude towards me as being more
Christian than many in Ireland', a reaction echoed by some
who do return and find in journalist Mary Kenny's phrase,
that 'while the Irish may give a welcome to strangers, they
are not, in my experience, notably hospitable to returned
emigrants. An element of suspicion attaches to those who
return, with their moral attitudes in particular being scrutinized
for evidence of pollution by the notions prevailing abroad.'

After a few years' trail–blazing journalistic work in Ireland
Mary Kenny returned to London because 'being a career girl
I couldn't resist the challenge of the job I was offered as features
editor of the *Evening Standard* (she is one of the few women
to hold such a position in Fleet Street) and also because 'Ireland
can be intellectually stifling; you meet the same people over and
over again and have the same conversations repetitively. London
is more mind–expanding, and from an intellectual point of
view, it challenges you more.'

A comparable reaction, put by a twenty-three-year-old girl
from a city in provincial Ireland, was that: 'I had to get out, or
burst. I couldn't take the heavy moral "respectability"; to be
frank, I couldn't express myself sexually; I was afraid that if I
stayed I would have ended up marrying some fellow I went out
with for a few years and spend the rest of my life wondering
what I might have missed. So all in a week I decided, drew
fifty pounds out of the bank, which I blew in two weeks of
sightseeing in London.' After that she took a flat in Bayswater,
a well–paid job, being a trained commercial artist, and a lover.
She vaguely holds the idea of returning home, but 'not for some
years yet. There's too much excitement for me here, finding out
about myself in the context of other people.'

She exemplifies the growing proportion of 'voluntary emigrants' of recent years who come for a variety of reasons other
than economic, and who bring with them no profound sense of
Irishness. But even among the bulk of semi–skilled and
labouring immigrants, the strong sense of Irishness is confined
to a minority and it is from this minority that the continuum of
racial awareness is transmitted through the generations. A
pointer to this degree of Irishness was revealed in a survey
carried out at a North London Catholic School in 1970, among

100 school children of Irish parentage, of whom 52 per cent regarded themselves as *neither* exclusively English or Irish, but 'a mixture of both', with the remaining 48 per cent dividing equally into English and Irish identifications of nationality. The figure of 62 per cent who had never attended any specific Irish club or function confirms the impression that a smaller proportion of immigrants participate in any outward declarations of Irishness, but in contrast (and perhaps in keeping with general emotional attachments) over half said they would cheer for Ireland in a football match against England.[30] This tenuous, if sporting, link with the land of their parents would seem to corroborate, and characterize the attitude of the majority of settled Irish, who for the most part would not wish their children to grow up with any stultifying extremity of Irishness, a view confirmed by the teacher who conducted the survey when he commented: 'Considering that most of the children have so far lived their lives in Britain, it is right that they should regard themselves as British; to go on regarding themselves as outsiders would only lead to future discontent and unhappiness.'

A more extreme report on being brought up in a strongly Irish—and Catholic—atmosphere in Britain was provided by writer John O'Callaghan.

To be brought up as an Irish Catholic in England is to be nurtured as a schizophrenic. I received an English education which may, I forget, have managed to include a sentence somewhere about the 1845 famine. History is the most obvious place to see first the effect of being introduced to a background of which I was not the true inheritor. In the flux of post–war schooling, class distinctions remained clear with public, grammar, and secondary modern schools giving appropriate training to the country's money, brains, and muscle.

Immigrant parents can be very isolated. Loving the material comforts, they lack the right social reflexes. So they—in my case—gave thanks for the blessings of escaping the milking stool in Clare by endorsing all the values of Clare. Sunday mass, serving one week–day mass, benediction, family rosary, these mechanisms of religious certainty were automatic. I was a kind of religious athlete in good trim.

Catholicism makes for one set of differences, while being Irish makes for another set; Irish people explode quicker, shout louder, sulk sooner than English. It was not until the sixth form that Irishness gained a status. And then it was the status of the acceptable Irish traits of humour, gab, directness and not the sad attributes of peevishness, deceit, and intractability. About this stage the brighter specimens recognized the shape of society, realized they would not come into its promised land as Irish creations. They honed up their accents, and bought a regimental tie.

But the Irish – the native Irish – presence of my parents at home brought reminders that the fair play, the self control, the impartiality of the British is as skin deep as in any other race. Hearsay at home of the Black and Tans, the Famine, Cromwell, shows the son of immigrants very early that things in England are not always what they seem. You are born outside furrows of thought that some pure natives never see over. It is worth risking the schizophrenia to be reared without blinkers.

'Risking the schizophrenia' may well characterize the endeavour of the Irish in Britain who, in spite of their increased cohesion, remain something of a neutered people, free of the full vigour of British life on the one hand, and of Irish life on the other.

Of Ireland, yet no longer living there. Of Britain now, yet not feeling British; geographically cut–off from the mainspring of their own native culture without being easily adaptable to the alternative one, they are nevertheless destined, however strident their protests, to be absorbed into the melting–pot of a multi-racial society. From whence, like the generations before them, the bones of their names will emerge in some future Labour cabinet, in trade unions, in the professions, and in every aspect of life in Britain.

Part Four

APPENDIX

Appendix

'Being Irish is a state of mind', wrote *Observer* journalist Patrick O'Donovan, born in Britain of an Irish doctor and M.P. Apart from temperamental inclinations, however, the legal definition of Irish rests with a multiplicity of enactments of the British and Irish Parliaments. The main source of recognition probably rests with the Irish Nationality and Citizenship Act of Dail Eireann of 1956, which specifies that:

Any person born in any part of Ireland is Irish and continues to be Irish, irrespective of where they live. The only exception to this is somebody who has formally taken nationality in another country.

Any person born in Northern Ireland after 1922 whose parents or grandparents were born anywhere in Ireland is Irish in the same manner as already specified.

Any person born in Northern Ireland after 1922 whose parents or grandparents were not born in Ireland may declare themselves Irish and have an Irish passport. Such people must sign an informal declaration giving details of date and place of birth and of current residence.

Anyone born in Britain, or elsewhere, of Irish parents or grandparents is entitled to Irish citizenship and an Irish passport on request.

The Irish constitution recognizes an individual's right to dual-nationality—although two passports may not be held at the one time.

HOW MANY PERSONS OF IMMEDIATE IRISH DESCENT IN BRITAIN?

It is difficult to compute a precise figure, but conservatively estimated at around four million, the principal pointer to this estimate being the figure of six million nominal members of the Roman Catholic religion in Britain, of which at least half may be reasonably held to be of immediate (first to third generation) Irish extraction. Bearing in mind the 'leakage' away from Roman Catholicism of a proportion of immigrants, and the fact that a minority are not, and were not, Catholics, plus the high fertility rate of Irish marriages (70 per cent above national average in 1966), the figure of four million Britons of Irish extraction may be taken as a reasonable approximation in round figures.

HOW MANY IRISH–BORN IN BRITAIN?

Over one million in round figures, or approximately 2 per cent of the population of Great Britain. The last available census figure, for 1966, declares a figure of 948,320 Irish–born in England, Wales, and Scotland. It is accepted by census officials that this figure may underestimate the true number, not least in the proportion of Irish–born who, for a variety of personal and financial reasons, are likely to have absented themselves during the visits of census enumerators. In the 'Population Census' by Bernard Benjamin, the author shows that a check survey held after the 1961 census revealed that the question of nationality was not answered by 'a significant proportion'. Thus a conservative estimate places the number of Irish–born at over one million.

WHERE DO THEY COME FROM IN IRELAND?

1966 Census:		
	from Irish Republic:	713,170
	from Northern Ireland:	209,530
	part of Ireland not stated:	25,620
		948,320

FROM WHAT REGIONS IN IRELAND?

Of the four provinces of Ireland—Leinster, Munster, Connacht, and Ulster—the western province of Connacht provides the highest proportion of immigrants to Britain. In the period 1966–71, for example, Connacht lost 10.6 persons per 1,000 of population, by contrast with the more industrialized eastern province of Leinster, which lost only 2.2 per 1,000. In the immediate post–Famine migrations of a century ago, the province of Munster lost the most people, with the highest number leaving the county of Cork. Today, the county of Leitrim in Connacht is the chief sufferer through emigration.

WHERE DO THEY SETTLE IN BRITAIN?

Principally in urban areas; in the principal towns Irish–born constitute approximately one in forty of the population.

HOW DO THEY COMPARE IN SOCIO–ECONOMIC STATUS TO THE NATIVE POPULATION?

Abstracts from the 1966 Census show that, among samples of economically–active males, the contrast was:

	Born in Ireland	Born in England and Wales
Professional workers	1.0%	3.1%
Employers and Managers	3.6%	8.3%
Non–Manual	13.2%	22.1%
Skilled Manual	36.5%	39.6%
Semi–skilled Manual	19.7%	15.7%
Unskilled Manual	24.8%	9.9%

HOW DO THE IRISH–BORN COMPARE WITH COLOURED (COMMONWEALTH) IMMIGRANTS?

Both immigrant groups are almost equal in numbers at around one million each. The Irish generally follow better–paid occupations than coloured immigrants, live in better housing conditions, and on average have more children per family at 2.52 children, as against an average of 2.24 children for coloured immigrant families.

One notable difference is that of sex–composition; unlike coloured immigrant groups where men predominate over women, the Irish hold a ratio of 912 males to every 1,000 females.

Comparing the three communities of Irish, coloured, and native British, available abstracts from the 1961 and 1966 Census suggest that: (1) the Irish approximate most to the native British community in areas of employment, housing, and education. (2) The Irish are most like the coloured community in areas of family size. (3) In areas of 'social problems', i.e. criminal offences, the Irish have a higher proportion than either native or coloured communities.

The general trend of Irish immigration to Britain, computed from various sources.* Allowing for margins of error in in-

* Returns of the Irish Registrar-General, British Census, British Home Office figures on Insurance and Social Welfare cards since 1948, *Commission on Emigration, Dublin* 1954

dividual years, due to inadequate or conflicting records, this graph nevertheless records the general trend of the Irish Diaspora to Britain since the Great Famine of 1845–47.

Although the Irish had come to Britain since earliest times, the successive famines of the early 1800s gave impetus to the tradition, culminating in the exodus from the Great Famine of 1845–47. During that period, and in the years immediately following, upwards of a quarter of a million a year came to Britain; around half of that number subsequently went to further destinations overseas, mainly America and Australia.

Acknowledgements and Sources

Apart from the miscellaneous reading matter later credited, the author is indebted to:

Hutchinson & Co., London, for permission to quote from *Borstal Boy*, by Brendan Behan (1958); *The Railway Navvies* by Terry Coleman, (1965).

McGibbon & Kee, London, for permission to quote from *With Breast Expanded* by Brian Behan, 1964.

Martin, Brian and O'Keefe for the quotation from *The Green Fool*, by Patrick Kavanagh, London, 1972.

Elspeth Kyle and the Camberwell Council on Alcoholism for the interview in Chapter 8.

Mr Patrick Mulloy, London, for use of the postcard from Bernard Shaw, quoted in Chapter 5.

Runnymede Industrial Unit, London, and author Shelley Markham, for quotations from the pamphlet '*What About the Irish?*' (1971).

The library staffs of the British Museum; Catholic Central Library, London; the Institute of Race Relations, London; The Irish Club, and Irish Embassy, London.

A debt is also owed to Noel O'Connell, distinguished engineer and amateur historian, who provided able direction in researching the post-Famine settlements and to Marie McGibbon (née Brock) whose original thesis on the aftermath of one such settlement—the Stockport Riots—was invaluable.

For insight into conditions in the building industry of the 1930s, I am indebted to the recently deceased Dominic Donnelly and for first-hand accounts of strikes in that same industry in the fifties, I am grateful to Brian Behan, Jack Henry, John Palmer, Pat O'Donovan.

Many people helped me in examining 'social problems' among the present-day Irish, including Maura Dorgan, C. D. Hunt, Fathers Sheridan and O'Donnell; others, who wish to remain anonymous, were equally informative. Further specialized knowledge of the Irish was provided by James Cantwell, James Kirby, Richard Kershaw, Paul Dwyer, Henry Harris.

Brendan Mac Lua of the *Irish Post* was a mine and monitor of information and unfailingly patient in answering a stream of enquiries. Able research assistance was provided by Carol Lazebrey, Margaret O'Connor, William Pinching, Jillian Orr. All are of course absolved from any conclusions which may appear contentious, but I cannot absolve them from their generous assistance in making the work possible.

KEVIN O'CONNOR
London 1972

Bibliography

The following works were consulted:

The British, by Drew Middleton, Secker & Warburg, London 1957

The British General Election, 1970, by David Butler and Michael Pinto–Duschinsky, Macmillan, London 1971

Catholic Emancipation 1829–1929, by Bernard Ward, Longmans, London 1929

Catholic London A Century Ago, by Bernard Ward, The Catholic Truth Society, London 1905

Commission on Emigration and Other Population Problems, Dublin 1954

The East End of London, by Millicent Rose, Cresset Press, London 1951

An Economic History of Britain, by Graham Turner, Eyre & Spottiswoode, London 1966

The English Catholics 1850–1950, ed. by George Andrew Beck, Burns Oates, London 1950

Geography of Greater London, ed. by Clayton, George Philip, London 1964

The I.R.A., by Tim Pat Coogan, Pall Mall Press, London 1970 (Fontana paperback edition, 1971)

Irish Immigrants in Manchester, 1830–54, unpublished thesis by Miss M. Brock, University of Southampton, 1962

The Irish in Britain, by John Archer Jackson, Routledge & Kegan Paul, London 1964

The Irish in Modern Scotland, by James E. Handley, Cork University Press, 1947

The Irish in Scotland, by James E. Handley, Cork University Press, 1943

An Irish Navvy, by Donall MacAmblaigh, Routledge & Kegan Paul, London 1964

Liverpool, by Mary Cathcart Borer, Longmans, London 1970

London Labour and the London Poor, by Mayhew, London 1861

Michael Collins, by Margery Forester, Sidgwick & Jackson, London 1970

The Railway Navvies, by Terry Coleman, Hutchinsons, London 1965 (Pelican paperback edition, 1968)

The R.C.'s, by George Scott, Hutchinsons, London 1964

The Second World War, by Winston Churchill, six volumes, Educational Book Co., London 1946–8

What About The Irish? Information Paper of the Runnymede Trust, by Shelley Markham, London 1971

With Breast Expanded (with a dedication to 'money and flat-chested women'), by Brian Behan, McGibbon & Kee, London 1964

Various pamphlets and Annual Reports of the Irish Centre, Camden Town (during the sixties), and of the Anti–Partition League (during the fifties)

Various journals, periodicals, and British and Irish newspapers

Text Notes

1. *Liverpool*, by Mary Cathcart Borer, Longmans, London 1971.
2. *The Railway Navvies*, by Terry Coleman, Hutchinson, London 1965.
3. Lord Bowes.
4. In St Albans in 1860, £5,700 *in pennies* had been contributed to the church building fund.
5. From an original but unpublished thesis, by Maire Brock, University of Southampton, 1962.
6. An indication of the massive inflow of the Irish into mid nineteenth-century Britain is the frequency with which the terms, Newtown or Irishtown occur in areas of major habitation.
7. Thesis by Brock.
8. *Catholic Emancipation*, Longmans, London 1928.
9. Liberal party 335 seats; Conservative 249 seats; balance 85 seats. Irish Parliamentary party 85 seats; + T. P. O'Connor's 1, 86 seats.
10. Although every generation since the Famine influx managed to produce a newspaper or periodical, most were short-lived. Many catered for a region, such as the *Irish Tribune* which circulated in the Newcastle area, or the *Irish Banner* in Scotland, and *Observer* in Glasgow which survived for a number of years. Only one, the *Catholic Herald* survives a century later, although no longer specifically Irish but catering to the British Catholic community at large.
11. J. T. Murphy, Tom Bell, Arthur McManus.
12. Christian Brothers, a religious order of stern disciplinarians which has dominated the primary and secondary education of most Southern Irish males during the past century.
13. The 'push–pull' syndrome of Irish immigration to Britain i.e., the movement of migratory labour from a static economy to a dynamic economy was now consolidated by the creation of the Welfare State during the Labour Government. By the end of 1946 the National Health Act, the National Insurance Act, and the National Assistance Act had been initiated, thereby radically upgrading the lot of the working classes generally and incidentally providing another powerful 'pull' factor upon Irish immigration to Britain.
14. The list of occupations of the founders of the Eaton Square Club is expressive of the emergent post-war, middle–class grouping of immigrants, ranging from the new–rich builders and businessmen to the more traditionally wealthy Anglo–Irish landowners, with the inevitable sprinkling of British Army personnel. *Founder Members, 1948*: H. Block, hotel proprietor; T. A. Crawford–Young; the Baron de Robeck, Army brigadier; John Dolan, businessman;

Dominick Donnelly, company director; David Duff Frame, company director; Matthew Gallagher, building contractor; Michael Gormon, dance hall proprietor; Jack P. Gleeson, building contractor; Norman Goodbody, company director; Denis Guiney, department store owner (Dublin); Tom Hickey, journalist; P. J. Kelly, bookmaker; John Kenny, company director; Eileen Kilgallin, legal executive; Lord Killanin, M.B.E.; James Labor, hotel proprietor; Lord Lurgan; Charles McConnell, chairman of advertising agency; Joseph McGrath, company director; Joseph McDonagh, civil servant; Dr Dan McLaughlin, medical practitioner; Patrick Mulloy, civil servant; Harold Murray, company director; Bryan O'Connor, solicitor; Nicholas O'Dwyer, company director; Lord Oronmore and Browne, landowner; Noel Purcell, actor; Philip Sayers; Michael Scott, F.R.I.A.I., architect; Captain Eustace Scott, former British Army officer; Michael Smyth, B.Sc., F.R.C.S., surgeon; Mrs Wilson Talbot; John Tate (Co. Dublin); Robert Thompson, peace commissioner; William Walsh, company director; Samuel Thornton.

15. *Defence Secretary*, Denis Healey; *Home Secretary*, James Callaghan; *Foreign Secretary*, George Brown; in the Labour Government of 1964–66 (during which George Brown was Minister of Employment and Productivity) and 1966–70. The three cabinet positions are, after the positions of Prime Minister and Chancellor, the next in order of influence. Of the three, George Brown made the most public declarations of his immediate Irish ancestry, particularly on Ulster matters and when faced with 'provocative' company such as powerful elements of the Foreign Office who were Anglo–Irish. The Opposition Leader, Edward Heath, (now Conservative Prime Minister) liked to refer to James Callaghan as 'the Welshman with an Irish name'. Defence Secretary Healey was more circumspect, although at a St Patrick's Day function in the Hilton Hotel in 1969, he regaled his audience with stories of his own 'Rebel Cork' background, describing how some of the first songs he learned were seditious sagas from his Irish father. In common with George Brown, Healey's father was of Cork origin.

16. *Irish Post* survey, 11 June 1970: sample 4,627, showing Irish voted 84:16 in favour of Labour. This confirms various studies since 1920. A study of electoral attitudes in the London borough of Greenwich in 1956 showed the Roman Catholic vote to be 70 per cent in favour of Labour.

17. *The British General Election, 1970*, by David Butler and Michael Pinto–Duschinsky, Macmillan, London 1971.

18. SHAC—apt initials for Shelter Housing Advisory Centre, which revolutionized the possibility of home ownership for the poorer sections of the community and intruded upon the house monopoly of the building societies. Presently run by a Dublin priest, Father Byrne, but its activities by no means confined to the Irish. An offspring of Catholic Housing Aid Society — see Chapter 8.

19. *Crimes of Violence*, by F. H. McLintock, Macmillan, London 1963.

20. *Crime, Police and Race Relations*, a study in Birmingham by John Lambert, Oxford University Press 1970.

21. *Commission on Emigration and other Population Problems*, 1948–54, Stationery Office, Dublin.

22. Most police officers and social workers with whom I discussed 'the Irish as a Social Problem' agree that this is an area of diminishing interest to them. There used to be a time ten years ago, when police stations in Irish districts assigned extra personnel at weekends outside Irish dance–halls and clubs. Police, in particular, say that disturbances are now numerically less and note the decreased posting of the 'Paddy Wagon' (police van) outside Irish recreational premises. The very title of 'Paddy Wagon' indicates the one–time position of Irish immigrants in police consciousness.

23. Special tabulations from the Census of 1961 *and* 1966 show that out of seven ethnic groups studied, the Irish have: the greatest number of children per family (2.52); the highest percentage of families with three or more children (42 per cent).

24. Catholic Housing Aid is now part of the SHELTER welfare umbrella, but retains its independent working–force. In 1971 it housed around 1,600 families, of which 193 were classed as 'fatherless families'.

25. 'The Return of the Venereal Diseases', *British Medical Journal*, 23 June 1962.

26. *Irish Times*: various issues October–November 1971.

27. The *Guardian*, 19 May 1971.

28. London has around twenty agencies and centres devoted to the care of the alcoholic. But given the disproportionately high number of clients of Irish origin, it is notable that at the time of writing only *one* of these is Irish–sponsored. Anyone interested in further research into this area of human misery could usefully contact Alcoholics Anonymous at 11 Redcliffe Gardens, London, S.W.10, or the Medical Council on Alcoholism who maintain an information advisory centre in London.

29. The *Sunday Times*, 5 December 1971.

30. *Irish Post* 23 December 1970.